THE 17 IRISH MARTYRS

ABOUT THE AUTHOR

MARY MCALEESE was born in Belfast, Northern Ireland in 1951. In 1975, she became Reid Professor of Criminal Law, Criminology and Penology at Trinity College Dublin, and in 1987 she was appointed Director of the Institute of Professional Legal Studies at Queen's University Belfast. She became the first female Pro-Vice Chancellor of Queens in 1995. She was elected President of Ireland in 1997. After stepping down as President in 2011, she earned a Licentiate and PhD in Canon Law from the Pontifical Gregorian University in Rome.

The —
17 IRISH
MARTYRS

MARY MCALEESE

columba
BOOKS

First published in 2022 by

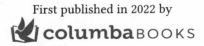 columbaBOOKS

Block 3b, Bracken Business Park,
Bracken Road, Sandyford,Dublin 18, D18 K277
www.columbabooks.com

ISBN: 978-1-78218-378-5

Set in Adobe Garamond Pro 11/15
Cover and book design by Maria Soto | Columba Books
Art Direction by Alba Esteban | Columba Books

Cover image:
Torturing and hanging of Dermot O'Hurley, Archbishop of Cashel,
A.D. 1584. Execution of Cornelius O'Devany, Bishop of Down and
Connor, and Patrick O'Lochran. Engraving, 1588. British Museum,
Public domain, via Wikimedia Commons

Printed by L&C, Poland.

This book is dedicated to the memory of a saintly woman, Bridget McDrury.

CONTENTS

INTRODUCTION

On 27 September 1992, His Holiness Pope John Paul II beatified sixteen Irishmen and one Irish woman. Each was a victim of Ireland's tempestuous history. Each one consciously chose to die a martyr rather than deny their faith in the Catholic Church. A bemused twentieth century Ireland was struck by the familiar echoes in the stories of the seventeen, each of whom had waited at least three centuries for recognition and celebration. I became interested in their stories when I was asked to be the presenter of a film about their lives and the better I got to know each of them the more aware I became of the reality that I and my contemporaries in Northern Ireland were still living out the dreadful consequences of those far-off times in which the martyrs lived. *Our* divisions, political and religious, were their divisions, *our* unhealed wounds, their wounds. How many generations of Christians were to continue this dreadful conflict? Was there one which could muster all its resources of political imagination and spiritual generosity and finally lay to rest all those ghosts. I hope so, and I hope it has finally arrived.

"Martyrdom represents the most perfect act of charity" says Thomas Aquinas: The Second Vatican Council agrees. In its document on the Dogmatic Constitution of the Church, "Lumen Gentium", the council states:

"From the earliest times ... some Christians have been called upon and some will always be called upon, to give this supreme testimony of love to all men, but especially to persecutors. The Church, therefore, considers martyrdom as an exceptional gift and as the highest proof of love. By martyrdom a disciple is transformed into an image of his Master, who freely accepted death, on behalf of the world's salvation; he perfects that image even to the shedding of blood."

Ireland is well acquainted with the shedding of blood, in its past and in its present. The seventeen now 'Blessed' martyrs lived during the worst of times, in that grim century of the three monarchs, Elizabeth I, James I and Charles I, culminating in Oliver Cromwell's bloody campaign against the Catholic Irish.

The words 'Ireland' and 'religious conflict' seem to have been synonymous for centuries. Before there was ever a religious conflict there was a political one, still resonating even now at the beginning of the twenty-first century; but in the sixteenth century the long and complex struggle of the Irish people against English imperial domination was given a new and bitter impetus when, in the wake of the Protestant Reformation, a large measure of religious strife was added to an already lethal political cocktail.

Many died in the ensuing turmoil, but not all were martyrs. Often they were angry men and women who took to arms to defend their property, their homes, their faith, or their country. Thousands died, their names forgotten with the passage of time. The martyrs were different. That revered title is awarded to those who died simply for their faith and for no other reason. No taint of militarism or vengeance touched their lives. They were the blameless victims of sectarian hatred.

Every cause has had its martyrs. No one religion, no one cause has a monopoly on martyrdom. The cause for which the martyrs in this book died was the freedom to believe in and practise the Roman Catholic faith in Ireland. Other martyrs died for their faiths at the hands of Catholics. All such savagery has had a long shelf-life skewing relationships right to the present day.

Europe of the sixteenth and seventeenth centuries was a maelstrom of religious wars which reflected little credit on any side, whether Catholic or Protestant. Where one or other held the reins of power, they were both equally capable of unspeakable cruelty. Both claimed that God was exclusively on their side. This God was of course the one God, in whom all protagonists professed to believe and was presumably therefore the same God! Whichever side he was on, this vengeful, murdering, bloodthirsty God bore scant resemblance to the gentle carpenter from Nazareth who counselled, no, commanded, his followers to love one another and love their enemies. Love was in scarce supply it seems during those horrific years and what there was, was reserved for 'ones own'. These were the years of the sectarian headcount, each side intent on outnumbering the other by foul means, or more unlikely, fair. God was re-created in man's image and likeness, a bully, small, petty and vindictive. Yet in the lives of the martyrs another image filters through; the image of a immense God, big enough to love both martyr and tormentor, a God of forgiveness capable of healing the wounds inflicted by so many of his creation on each other, and in his name.

How does one explain in a few paragraphs the background of the lives to these seventeen? What happened to them corrupted the course of Irish history, making their story and the myths and legends of their contemporaries the fuel on the fire of contemporary Ireland. It is important to avoid being partisan when the sectarian, hate-filled politics of Reformation and Counter-Reformation still can spew their venom four hundred years away from their historical source, and particularly when one has lived slap bang in the middle of them. That is not the intention. This is the simple storytelling of the history of some of the people who shaped my ancestors and the faith they handed down through generations of suffering, a suffering they could at any time have cast off by abandoning their faith, as many did. But they did not. Today, their Church faces many new challenges, not least those induced by its own institutional weakness, its failures, betrayals, and its vanity. Yet it was this same Church these martyrs died for. If it survives today then it does so, at least partly, because of the sacrifices made by its faithful who over centuries of doubt and repression drew comfort and strength and bolstered their flagging faith by remembering the courage of the martyrs. Maybe some of today's antagonisms can make more sense in the light of these stories and their historical context.

If I tell you the whole sorry business started with the first and the only ever English Pope, I am not, I hope, making a biased political statement but a reasonable judgement call, made with the benefit of considerable hindsight. Adrian IV became Pope in 1154. In the five years he sat on the throne of Peter he kept the Holy Spirit thoroughly preoccupied with wars and political intrigue. If he were infallible he kept the evidence of it well hidden. Among his more notorious blunders was the granting to Henry II of the papal Bull (aptly named) *Laudabiliter* under which he the Pope gave to the King of England the island known as Ireland. The fact that it wasn't his to give escaped his notice, though not that of historians to whom he gave a numerous field days. That started it - England's assertion of ownership over Ireland, still disputed today, some nine hundred years later.

For the first four hundred years or so, it was a straight fight between the Crown and the native Irish, with a dizzy kaleidoscope of changing alliances and internecine falling-outs which ensured that England never fully subdued the country and the Irish never clearly won it back. Then in the early 1500s came the Reformation. At first, the critical tensions it raised left Ireland untouched, but after Henry VIII's squabble with Rome about the status of his marriage to Catherine of Aragon, England was ripe for conversion to Protestantism. An embittered monarch and his successors established Anglicanism not just as a State Church but as the only acceptable church for all people under their dominion. Catholics in England were persecuted and martyred and attention turned to Ireland. How ironic that the successor of Henry II, who had been given Ireland as a papal gift, should now be the author of a plan designed to wipe every trace of Roman Catholicism from the map of Ireland.

Practice of the faith was part of the warp and weft of daily life throughout Ireland. A strong monastic tradition, allied to a Celtic spirituality, gave the Irish their characteristic and unique expression of faith. They weren't an overly pious people, however, there is plenty of evidence of the manifest human weakness of some of their spiritual leaders but they became a Mass-going people and in the century before the Reformation many new churches were built and friaries established.

They were however, a curiously unpredictable people. In England, when the Government made the practice of the Catholic faith too dangerous an occupation for all but the most devoutly defiant, and an ominous amount of Catholic blood had been spilt, the terrorised population obliged the Monarch by embracing the new state religion more or less en masse. The Irish were made of entirely different stuff, as successive English administrations were to discover to their cost.

The campaign to rid Ireland of Catholicism started out benignly enough at first, but as resistance grew and practice of the Catholic faith remained as fresh and enthusiastic as ever, the government tightened the screws. Within a relatively short space of time attendance at Mass was outlawed, attendance at Protestant services was made compulsory, Catholic priests were banished and the remotest trace of Roman Catholic practice was likely to result in imprisonment at best and summary execution at worst. Like a gathering storm, the repression of Catholicism grew more and more punitive. People attended mass in secret hideaways. They travelled miles to rendezvous with fugitive priests to receive the sacraments, and went for months on end with no access to confession, communion, confirmation, marriage, and last rites. Young men entering the priesthood had to go abroad to France, Belgium or Spain to receive their education. Catholic institutions of learning were outlawed. When the ordained priests came home to Ireland, it was to the misery of a life on the run, sneaking in disguise from safe house to safe house, always vulnerable to betrayal, for Ireland had more than its fair share of willing informers. For over one hundred years, the penalty for being a Catholic in Ireland was the threat and often the reality of violent death. In subsequent centuries, the penalty would be a series of crippling social, economic and political disabilities which affected the lives of Catholics not only in Ireland but in imperial Britain most but not all of which are now dismantled.

In each generation there were many who sacrificed their lives for their faith. Their contemporaries were not easily fooled. They knew the difference between the innocent martyr and the political activist, and while they might fully sympathise with the latter and while the latter might suffer as many tortures and indignities as the martyr, they were unlikely to attribute to them the title 'martyr'. The evidence of the times strongly supports the view that the reputation of martyrdom was reserved with great circumspection for those whose lives held up to the clearest scrutiny. Only one such Irish martyr has ever been canonised, Saint Oliver Plunkett, the last Bishop to die for his faith, martyred at Tyburn, London in 1681. He was beatified in 1920 and canonised in 1975. Yet Irish folklore abounded with the stories of literally hundreds of other martyrs, and their names would not go away. Over the centuries they nagged relentlessly at the conscience of scholars and researchers. Trawling through a forest of historical documentation straddling many countries and only haphazardly recorded was a formidable task but it began in earnest in the middle of the nineteenth century when Father Patrick Moran, drawing on the work of seventeenth century martyrologists, uncovered much that had lain dormant in Vatican archives. In fits and starts work on the martyrs' cause trundled on into the new century. On 18 February 1904 a tribunal was set up in Dublin to examine the cases of some four hundred and sixty reputed martyrs. By the end of the year, eighty sessions had been held and the number of martyrs had been reduced to 292. A further enquiry was held in Dublin in 1907 and after laborious critiquing of the available evidence, 257 cases were admitted in 1915 by the Sacred Congregation of Rites. They were now on the first rung of a very long and precarious ladder. In 1917 an Apostolic Process (enquiry) opened in Dublin into these causes. The task confronting the members of the enquiry was utterly formidable. A team of eighty people worked on it, producing almost 40,000 pages of written material within eighteen months. They ran out of money. Hardly surprising. More fits and more starts followed until in 1936 an entirely sensible cleric Father Antonelli confronted with an uncontrollable mass of paperwork shouted halt and strongly advised that the only intelligent way forward was to select the strongest and best documented cases, and concentrate only on those. Twenty years later the Archbishop of Dublin, John Charles McQuaid, took Antonelli's advice, but it was his successor Archbishop Dermot Ryan who in 1975 brought the entire matter under control when he appointed a Diocesan Commission for Causes. The efforts of this dedicated group of historical scholars produced two enormous tomes (known as The Positio) of distilled and convincing evidence to substantiate the causes of the seventeen people whose stories are told here. No sooner had their work borne fruit in the beatification of the seventeen, than they resumed their work on the next group.

The Positio is the primary source for this book. What was it about these seventeen that gave them the stamp of martyrdom? They were not all priests, among them are lay people from many walks of life. They were born into an Ireland in the vicious grip of the Penal Laws, described colourfully and accurately by Edmund

Burke as a "machine of wise and elaborate contrivance, as well fit-ted for the oppression, impoverishment and degradation of a peo-ple and the debasement in them of human nature itself as ever pro-ceeded from the perverted ingenuity of man." The martyrs resisted their debasement not with violence but with their faith. Accused of being loyal to the Pope, they admitted it. Offered freedom, money and status if they transferred their spiritual loyalty to the Monarch, they refused. Tortured to induce them to recant, they prayed for forgiveness for their torturers and remained steadfast in their faith, even as they mounted the scaffold to death. Impressive witness-es? Perhaps they still have something important to say to a world where faith is at times a fickle thing, so different from the diamond hard vision of a loving God forged in the souls of those martyrs through the crucible of suffering on a scale we can only imagine and thank God we do not have to face. Our peers in other parts of the world are not so fortunate. Today, people still die for their faith. The long history of the Jewish people is one of persistent per-secution, none more barbarous, more debased than the genocide visited upon them in the twentieth century. They were martyred in their millions, changing the face of the earth yet again. Today, the names of Israel and Palestine conjure up images of a vicious con-temporary conflict in which the word "martyr" is often heard, and it is far from absent in the language of international terrorism. It is a word with deep significance and ramifications, a prized status, an icon drawing new generations to the call of its cause. A word to be careful with, to be wary of, to judge well, for it is claimed also by fools and knaves. However we remember and whatever our view of those who claim the name, may we in remembering these few of Ireland's martyrs, have compassion for one and all, torturer and tortured, all the casualties of history. Even more importantly, may we who claim to be Christians find the unconditional forgiveness to have love even and especially for the misguided men and women who visited such cruelty on their brother and sister human beings. It is relatively easy to flood our hearts with sorrow and righteous indignation for the martyrs. However, the true test of our Christian identity will be our ability to find loving forgiveness for their betrayers and killers, in fact to forgive the history we inherited and decide to build a new history where Christians do in fact love one another no matter what and in spite of everything.

CHAPTER 1

Patrick O'Healy, O.F.M. and Conn O'Rourke, O.F.M.

Martyred 1579

History is selective about the memories it cherishes. Generations of young Catholic Irish people today are familiar with the story of the martyrdom of St. Oliver Plunkett, Archbishop of Armagh, who was executed at Tyburn in 1681. Yet in many ways his was the end of a much longer story, for he was the last Irish Bishop to die for his faith during more than a century of violent religious repression. The first was Patrick O'Healy, Bishop of Mayo.

It is sobering to reflect that if Patrick O'Healy were to find himself suddenly transported to twenty-first century Europe, he would have little difficulty in updating himself on certain contemporary problems. From the Troubles in Northern Ireland, to the assertion of Catalan identity, there would be little that would be unfamiliar to his eyes. For this holy man of outstanding intellect and spirituality was as much at home in the harsh wilds of County Leitrim as he was in the opulence of the Spanish Church.

Experts differ on the precise place and date of Patrick O'Healy's birth, but he entered the world around 1543, probably in County Sligo in north-western Ireland, where the O'Healy clan (O'hEllidhe in Gaelic) was strong. Events in England in the decade preceding his birth were to cast a long and ominous shadow over his life, and indeed life in Ireland generally, for centuries to come.

From 1169, the English monarchy had struggled with more failure than success to bring a fragmented and hostile Ireland under its imperial domination. For almost four hundred years it was a classic political struggle for power and influence, but in 1534 a new and provocatively combustible element was added. The reigning monarch, Henry VIII, turned against Papal authority, created the Church of England and set himself up as its Supreme Head on earth. It was a remarkable turnabout for a king who had only a few years earlier loudly denounced Luther, and earned for himself the papal title, "Defender of the Faith." The immediate cause of the break with Rome was the Pope's refusal to annul Henry's first marriage to Catherine of Aragon, the widow of Henry's brother Arthur. The marriage had produced a daughter, Mary, but Henry badly wanted a son to ensure constitutional stability. With considerable theological ingenuity, he concluded that his marriage to Catherine was incestuous since she had been his brother's wife. The Pope refused to agree, for reasons which were both political and moral. Henry had meanwhile found a replacement for Catherine in the shrewd but ill-fated Anne Boleyn. He procured a civil divorce from Catherine without Papal approval, and so set in motion a catalogue of cathartic historical consequences. Not the least of these was the encouragement of the Protestant Reformation, an objective ironically as far from Henry's heart as it was from the Pope's. Of such quirks is history often made and its course distorted.

Henry's reign became synonymous with violence, moral degradation and schism. In an orgy of blood, the monasteries were dissolved and their wealth transferred to the Crown. He distributed the monastic lands as rewards to his chief supporters, thereby creating a class of new landowners who would resist any settlement with the Church.

The break with Rome was to have substantially different out-comes in Ireland and England. In the latter, the new State Church by dint of pressure and persuasion, became absorbed into the broad national landscape so that Romanism rapidly developed a minority status. Ireland, however, was an entirely different matter. The new religion was seen as yet another part of an ongoing programme of English political domination. Just as the latter had been resisted for generations, so would its latest manifestation. New laws criminalis-ing allegiance to Rome went largely unheeded. Even among many of those who were otherwise loyal to the English Crown, there was a hostility to accepting the new religion. The same dilemma had cost the life of Henry's Chancellor, Sir Thomas More. His devo-tion to the King as Head of State was never in doubt, but it was not enough. His staunch refusal to accept any other head of the Church except the Pope was interpreted as High Treason. Many others were to die in England and Ireland accused of being traitors in the same circumstances.

The O'Healy household doubtless took some comfort in the re-instatement of Roman Catholicism when Henry's daughter Mary assumed the throne in 1553. Although she would still, as English monarch, find little allegiance outside the Pale (an area around Dublin from which English rule over Ireland was dispensed), yet her attempted and ultimately unsuccessful rout of Protestantism in England created respite for the Catholic faith in Ireland, and it was during that temporary lull that Patrick O'Healy grew to adolescence. The lull lasted five short years. It was followed by a century of terror.

Mary's half-sister, Elizabeth, the daughter of Anne Boleyn, be-came Queen in 1558. The two had not exactly been models of sisterly affection.

For Mary, stuck with the ignominious label of 'incest', legiti-macy and recognition lay with Rome, while that same Rome was the very source of doubt about the legality of Elizabeth's parents' marriage. Now that Elizabeth was monarch, the pendulum swung forcefully back towards Protestantism.

To make England Protestant was a relatively easy if ignominiously achieved task. The treatment of English Catholics, after an initial rapprochement, grew worse and finally murderously grim after a papal interdict against Elizabeth in 1570. The Papal Bull, entitled "Regnans in Excelsis," was tantamount to a declaration of war against Elizabeth. She was formally excommunicated, but more importantly she was deemed to be deposed. Her subjects were told that they need no longer be loyal to her. In the eyes of the Pope England was a fief of the Holy See, ruled over by an illegitimate and thus disinherited monarch. The effect was only to help copperfasten the link between patriotism and Protestantism.

In Ireland however, Elizabeth had yet to subdue the country politically, never mind attempting to subdue it theologically. So great were the obstacles to both that they were not consistently followed through until after 1570, when ruthless coercion ensured that by the end of Elizabeth's reign all political opposition had either fled or been decimated. England's military and political control of Ireland was complete by the turn of the century, but the political success failed to guarantee theological success. No matter how ruthless the insistence that Ireland adopt the new State Church, the Irish resisted. The martyrs' role in that resistance was as pivotal as it was perplexing. The English authorities believed it was possible to terrify the people into subjection by imposing monstrously cruel deaths on well-known recusants. The Irish, far from becoming terrified, became outraged and defiant. Their hearts and minds would never be colonised, no matter what happened to their unfortunate country.

Patrick O'Healy was destined to become one of the most celebrated of the martyred recusants. He entered the priesthood shortly after Elizabeth became Queen. He had few illusions about the difficult life he was undertaking, but throughout his life his friends and acquaintances were in awe of his strength of character. One fellow priest who knew him well wrote: "... it was no wonder he was called Helium (to do with the sun) or O'Healy because he was on fire with incredible love ... He was like the sun shining its gleaming rays of virtue on others to set them on fire with zeal and piety ..." He would need every bit of that profound strength, for to be a Catholic was to invite trouble; to be a priest was to court death.

O'Healy joined the Observant Franciscan friary in Dromohaire, County Leitrim while still in his teens. The Observant friars had been in the forefront of the fifteenth century reform of the decaying monastic way of life in Ireland. It was in dire need of revitalisation, and the Observants' crusade for a return to piety and profound spirituality touched a nerve. Monastery after monastery adopted the Observant reforms, new monasteries were founded and a tremendous interest among lay people led to the spread of the Third Order of St. Francis. By the time Patrick became a friar, the Observant Franciscans were already as famed for their holiness as for their radical opposition to the Protestant Reformation.

The year 1561 saw Patrick installed in the remote monastery at Dromohaire as a novice, but he did not complete his training for the priesthood in Ireland. He was an excellent student who outshone his peers, and he soon found himself travelling abroad to continue his studies. He arrived in Rome in 1562, a young man of no more than nineteen and possibly as young as sixteen. The Minister General of the Observant Franciscans was a Spaniard, Francisco Zamora. The two met in Rome and Zamora was deeply impressed by the young Irish friar. He sent him to his own Spanish Franciscan province in Cartagena to develop his formation as a priest and scholar. Patrick spent two years studying grammar in the friary at Molina de Aragon and a further four years learning philosophy in San Clemente. From there he went to Cuenca and finally to the University of Alcala de Henares to complete his theological studies.

By then not only was he fluent in Catalan but he was acknowledged to be a man of deep spirituality and formidable intellect. He earned quite a reputation as a skilled debater, with a legendary reservoir of famous texts which he had committed to memory and could recall instantly. He was also passionately concerned about the fate of his country and his fellow Catholics. No good news would have reached him in Spain, for there was nothing good to tell.

The Ireland he had left behind was far from being a coherent nation. Allegiances were feudal and parochial. Clan fought against clan. The Anglo-Irish fought against the Gaelic. When it suited the Gaelic clan leaders to offer allegiance to the English monarch, they did so. When it suited them to betray one another, they did that too. When the Monarch became too intrusive into the lives of his subjects, they rebelled. Ireland was, in short, an ungovernable mess. The Irish Parliament was utterly ineffective, meeting only six times in the period from 1536 to 1603. Laws were generally imposed by royal proclamation over the heads of the Parliamentarians and executed when necessary by brutish and extensive martial law.

The new State-Protestant religion was in a parlous state in Ireland. Large parts of the country had never heard of it or had grown lax about practising it in the absence of serious commitment to its enforced implementation. In such an atmosphere, Catholic Counter-Reformation adherents were able to kindle a small but powerful movement. Simultaneously, political revolt was fomenting, occasionally erupting into open rebellion. The Tudor monarchs found themselves fighting off opposition on several fronts. In the South, the Desmond clan led a bitter four-year uprising in Munster. In the East, the Pale, the very symbol and heart of Tudor loyalty, was shaken to its core by a widespread anti-Tudor conspiracy. In the Northern province of Ulster the legendary chieftains O'Neill and O'Donnell spearheaded a campaign against the Crown, which threatened to engulf the entire country. Ireland was teetering on the brink of serious instability and, what was worse, the religious dimension of that instability was gaining in profile. Few of the rebels were imbued with single-minded religious zeal, but there were bonuses to be gained from using religion to justify resistance to the Crown. It unified the opposition, drawing more people into rebellion and most important of all, it opened up the prospect of help from the powerful Catholic nations, in particular from Philip II of Spain, whose relationship with Elizabeth had been explosive from the outset.

Patrick O'Healy was drawn inexorably into the climate of intrigue. A committed and educated Counter-Reformationist, he saw Ireland as an important battleground and he wanted to play his part. He was a passionate man of exceptional rhetorical skills. He began to put them to use for Ireland. By 1575, he was actively involved in trying to persuade the Spanish king and the Pope to help the cause of Catholics in Ireland. He had come to Rome to plead for approval of a plan, devised by the Gaelic Earl, James Fitzmaurice (a member of the Munster Desmond clan), to lead Irish Catholics in a war against the "heretical" Queen of England, and to replace her with a new monarch, Don Juan of Austria. Fitzmaurice had been a straightforward career soldier, deeply committed to the political defeat of the Crown in Ireland. In 1575, when his revolt ended in surrender to the Crown, he went abroad. It was in Rome that the swordsman became a committed Catholic crusader and embraced the ideology of the Counter-Reformation. It filled him with a new vision and determination to continue his fight against the Tudors only this time, whatever about the past, his was essentially a fight for the freedom to practise his Faith in the country of his birth. To O'Healy, Fitzmaurice offered hope, a commodity in short supply as Tudor repression tightened its grip over both Ireland and England.

O'Healy was well received in Rome where the Fitzmaurice scheme was regarded as far from being outlandish. The Pope recommended it to the King of Spain and sealed his approval of the young Irish monk by appointing him Bishop of Mayo on 4 July 1576. For the next year the new Bishop travelled between Madrid and Lisbon trying to get King Philip to firm up his support for Fitzmaurice. It was a wearisome and frustrating period, but his new status as a member of the hierarchy added to his powers of influence.

Progress was painfully slow. King Philip was not known as Philip the Prudent for nothing, though at times the anxious O'Healy may have thought the word 'prudent' a bit too charitable. Eventually his relentless lobbying seemed to pay off. On 14 November 1577 he wrote to Giovanni Francesco Mazza de Canobio, the Papal Collector, thanking him for his help in putting pressure on the Spanish Ambassador to Portugal to furnish Fitzmaurice, O'Healy and their colleagues with a ship to bring them to Ireland. They set sail four days later.

The journey was anything but uneventful. One setback followed upon another. The weather was so diabolical that the ship was unable to get beyond the Spanish coast for a full month. They had hoped to be in Ireland by then. O'Healy's faith in the enterprise must have been as sorely tested as his body was by the dreadful conditions on board. They limped into Bayonne for repairs and set sail again. Things were no better. The weather grew worse and they once more sought shelter in a Spanish port, this time in Monueiro, near Corunna. Three long nerve-wracking weeks were wasted there during which a serious dispute arose between Fitzmaurice and the ship's captain. The latter, a Breton, had had enough. He refused to take them any further and, along with his crew, was imprisoned for breach of contract. It was by now 6th January, the feast of the Epiphany. Fitzmaurice and O'Healy returned from Mass to find that the crew had broken out of prison. The ship and its cargo had set sail for Brittany without its illustrious passengers.

A fly on the wall of the quay in Monueiro might have heard some unbishoplike but understandable utterances, and yet these aggravations were only a minor apprenticeship for what O'Healy was to face later. They may well, however, have been an import- ant apprenticeship. Sick at heart, the two men made their way to France to try to retrieve their stolen property.

The details of their harrowing experiences were recounted by Bishop O'Healy in a long letter to the Pope's secretary of State, Tolomeo Cardinal Galli. Written from Paris on 31 March 1578, it shows that O'Healy's commitment and optimism suffered little in spite of overwhelming adversity. More importantly, it also shows his abhorrence of violence and his deep love of all humanity, even of 'the enemy'.

> When I left Portugal, I did not think that I would be writing to you until I reached the shores of Ireland. However, I am now writing from France, but I had imagined that I would be reporting good news from Ireland that a victory over the enemy of the Church had been achieved. It has turned out far differently.
>
> On the 18th of November we had just set sail from Lisbon heading for Ireland looking for a favour- able wind when we encountered an English ship. Our soldiers attacked it and captured it. We did not want human blood to be shed in front of a bishop and we wanted the enemy to experience kindness rather than harshness from the Duke so I asked Lord James to of- fer freedom to all the English if each of them in turn would take an oath of loyalty to the Apostolic See. Failing that, I asked him to send the spies to Spain accompanied by some of his own soldiers.
>
> We now began to set sail again on the intended route and when we were more than a month at sea we came up against a storm and hurricane force winds.

Finally we were compelled once again to seek the refuge of the Spanish coast. We spent twenty days there sheltering from the storm. Since our supplies began to run out, many of our soldiers left us.

A Church holy day occurred and all of us disembarked and went to Mass on land. Unknown to us, the captain along with the sailors sailed away. They left us without provisions, money or arms and took all our personal possessions away with them. They headed for home in Brittany. We pursued them to France, hoping to recover what we had lost. Lord James stayed in harbour at St. Malo.

I came to Paris to ask the king to order the restoration of what we had lost. The people who had robbed us, meanwhile, forewarned the Queen of England to look out for us and stop us getting to Ireland. I could not get a royal mandate for recovering our possessions.

We had to put up with all these setbacks. When Lord James got to Portugal, he discovered that there were no boats available to be bought, nor could he even hire an Italian or Spanish boat. He acted quickly in order to carry out the orders of His Holiness. He took a chance by travelling with some French sailors, bringing with him all his belongings, although he did not trust them very much. If I had gone to Rome a second time, I would have acted as interpreter for Lord James in his audience with His Holiness. One time before, I had got him an audience with the Pope and Lord James had got his request on the strength of my word. There is no way His Holiness would have offered the blessing of the Church to the plan (for the crusade) unless he backed it up with soldiers. He would not have wanted to see the authority of the Church appear weak or give his enemies a chance to mock us. Indeed, Lord James would never have departed from the Roman Curia unless he had hoped he would receive some protection in Portugal from a representative of the Apostolic See. He would show to this person the letters from your eminence which he had brought with him.

Once a task is undertaken, there should be no turning back if it is to work out right. Nothing should stop it – neither the honour of God, the authority of the Church, the judgement of the Holy See, the status of kingdoms, the safety of those close to us who should be more dear to us than life itself, the good of everyone, the state of the weather! We must go on. Lord James must be helped to get to Ireland. Now he is staying in Brittany, not expecting help from the most Christian King from whom he cannot look for anything or in whom he cannot put any hope. However, he is waiting for a helping hand from His Holiness. Unless he feels that this aid is prompt, there is a danger of the Holy See becoming discredited in the eyes of its enemies. Therefore, a task which had begun might turn out to be a source of shame for the Holy See because it could not finish it.

There is also a fear that all the Chieftains and noblemen of Ireland and the friends of Lord James may be put to death shortly unless he arrives as soon as possible. If this happens (God forbid), then the door will be closed to any other nations remedying the situation. Indeed the Queen of England, on hearing rumours of Lord James and Lord Stukely, is now persecuting the Catholics more severely and she has stationed many ships in the Irish harbours and her ships are also patrolling the open sea. Also, there is now a great chance of finishing the affair off once and for all because all the Scots who speak a language similar to our own (Gaelic) are joined with us in a treaty of friendship and they are very much up in arms. We have heard that three of the most powerful Gaelic princes, namely O'Neill, O'Donnell and O'Rourke, have risen in insurrection against the Queen of England. If Lord James were to arrive quickly, he would get plenty of assistance from them – there is great danger in delaying.

Two methods occur to me by which His Holiness can help Lord James.

One is to release a Papal Bull, directed in general terms at all the kings of Christendom and the princes and rulers of any nations, stating that if they were to give a helping hand to Lord James and to promote the cause of religion against the Queen of England, they would get a plenary indulgence remitting all their sins and saying, in strict terms, that anyone who hindered James for any reason from carrying out his task would be excommunicated.

The second alternative is that His Holiness would purchase the necessary arms and send them to Lord James (because for the sake of the country and of religion, not only the spiritual treasures of the Church but even the temporal ones should be opened up). If His Holiness was not prepared to do this, the task once begun would not have much success and everyone would be labouring in vain. Lord Stukely without the presence of Lord James could not achieve anything in Ireland, even if he were in charge of a thousand troops instead of the one hundred which he had with him. If Lord James could only have one ship, however many English ships there are running to and fro he and us along with him, in the name of God and by the power of the Holy See, will not hesitate nor be afraid of setting out for the fatherland and journeying to it once more. Since this is very important and requires the greatest speed, as soon as your Eminence gets these letters, I would like you to go and meet the Holy Father. Then we can have a reply as quickly as possible and we will then understand what to do.

Perhaps your Eminence will say either that I am more free in writing an equal or that I am doubtful of receiving help from His Holiness; but please remember that with the help of God's grace I shall be much more free and ready to give up life and blood and all I have, should need there be, for the safety and exaltation of the Apostolic See, for the propagation of the Catholic faith and the spread of the Christian religion and that I have every confidence in the bountiful goodness of His Holiness, which in experience I have found to be great and prompt. However necessity urges me on, the task in hand compels me, charity, zeal for religion and care for the salvation and safety of my brethren motivates me, and above all there is now the best chance of getting the thing completed successfully. I am writing with more urgency than usual because the cause is so necessary. I do not want to be seen distrusting the goodness of His Holiness. I am likewise writing to our Illustrious Protector (Cardinal Alciati) so both of you would act as pillars of the Church by raising the terrible yoke of slavery from our shoulders. Farewell.

Paris 31st March 1578.

To your Eminence
From your brother
Patrick-Bishop of Mayo.

O'Healy's influence and the respect in which he was held can be gleaned from the fact that he was ultimately successful in obtaining restitution of the stolen property and in extracting a further financial contribution of 1,000 gold crowns from the Pope. However, Cardinal Galli's prompt reply to this letter, while it promised help to Fitzmaurice if the expedition got going quickly, also provoked O'Healy to take a long hard look at his own role. To be an advocate for Lord James in those circles where he could have influence was one thing; to accompany him and his clearly military force was quite a different matter. Fitzmaurice eventually left Brittany for Spain to reorganise the expedition. But this time he left alone. O'Healy had not waned in his support for Fitzmaurice's plan, but he had now reevaluated his own direct involvement in it. He was after all a churchman, not a politician; a minister of the Gospel, not a soldier. His first and only ambition was to bring the Gospel to the people of Mayo. Correspondence between himself and the Vatican shows that the Pope too was concerned to see O'Healy's role as purely pastoral and that he wanted him to take up his appointment in Ireland as quickly as possible. The bishop saw that it was essential to clarify and remain true to his apostolic role. He therefore took no further part in Fitzmaurice's scheme. Instead, he stayed on in Paris for the best part of a year, living in the same Franciscan friary as the man who would become his first biographer, an English Franciscan named Thomas Bourchier.

Even there, he was plagued by problems. During the summer of 1578, another Irish Franciscan, Denis Molan, reported the Bishop's former involvement with Fitzmaurice's crusading plans to the English ambassador in Paris. O'Healy was outraged at this betrayal by a fellow Irishman and Franciscan. In strong language he denounced Molan to the papal nuncio and asked that Rome be warned of his behaviour. With O'Healy's connections it is likely that he was heeded.

These were confusing days for the bishop, but he settled into the busy daily routine of the seminary, taking a great deal of interest in the education of the young friars. He helped them with their studies, played games with them and showed a genuine concern for each one individually. He was a formidable presence, and yet he made time for everyone from the highest to the lowest. Passionate, intellectual, widely travelled and well-connected, he was something of a celebrity, but it was his holiness and humility which made a lasting impression on his colleagues and students. His object was still to make his way to Ireland, and in Paris he found the travelling companion who was to accompany him all the way to martyrdom, Conn O'Rourke.

Whether accident or design brought these two men together is impossible to say. Conn O'Rourke remains one of the most mysterious and enigmatic of the martyrs. Like O'Healy, he was from the Province of Connacht and had joined the Franciscans in Dromohaire some years after O'Healy had left for Spain. In fact, the monastery in that far western corner of County Leitrim had been founded by his grandparents in 1508. His family ties to the

Franciscans were longstanding, and while Conn O'Rourke was an illegitimate son (the canon law of marriage being largely ignored) he was an acknowledged nobleman, the son of the Gaelic chieftain Brian Ballach O'Rourke, said to be of more distinctive lineage than almost any contemporary royalty anywhere in Europe. He was about six years younger than O'Healy but would certainly have heard of the latter during his novitiate at Dromohaire. There was another, more intriguing, connection. The Tudor administration in Ireland employed spies to report on the movements of priests. One such report, dated 1577, claims that O'Rourke, recently arrived from Sligo, was living in Paris in lodgings paid for by one James Fitzmaurice. Given his noble background, Conn O'Rourke was more than likely very well versed in the politics of resistance and rebellion. At the Observant monastery he would have been an avid student of the Counter-Reformation. As a young man lately arrived from Ireland, he would also have been in no doubt about the dangers which awaited any priest returning to Ireland where the civil authorities were fomenting fury against Rome and Rome's adherents, which in the case of Ireland was almost the entire population of the island.

Following in the footsteps of O'Healy, Conn O'Rourke had gone abroad to continue his studies. With so much in common, and with O'Healy's hunger for up-to-date information about his homeland, it is possible to imagine the bond which developed between the two men. O'Healy had been away from home for many years. Here was a confrere right up to date on the situation and presumably with knowledge of the many friends O'Healy had left behind in Dromohaire and in Sligo. Nothing O'Healy heard would have comforted him. The political atmosphere in Ireland was worsening daily as the Government engaged in even harsher repression of Catholicism. If O'Healy had been eager to return a year earlier when he had set out with Fitzmaurice, he was now all the more eager to get back to assist his beleaguered people. Elizabeth's reign of terror against Catholicism was making life more intolerable daily.

O'Healy set off for Brittany with Conn O'Rourke in the hope of finding a suitable ship heading for Ireland. Little is known about their journey, possibly because O'Healy wanted as scant attention as possible from the ubiquitous Tudor spies. Their interest in him was not just with his links to Fitzmaurice. Of as much and probably more concern was the fact that as a Catholic bishop he might stir up disaffection from Elizabeth's State Church. The Tudor administration did not want any more bishops openly encouraging the practice of Catholicism. In any case, O'Healy had no knowledge of Fitzmaurice's revised plans, for the two men had been out of touch with each other for over a year.

Fitzmaurice, meanwhile, had the help of a new band of intermediaries with the Pope and the Spanish monarch, and had managed to put together an expeditionary force which set sail from Galicia in northwestern Spain on 20 June 1579. Several Franciscans accompanied him, among them the bishop of Killala, Donnchadh Og O'Gallagher.

Coincidentally, O'Healy and O'Rourke arrived in Smerwicke Haven, in a remote part of County Kerry, only a matter of weeks before Fitzmaurice sailed into the same harbour on 18 July 1579. Neither man had the foggiest idea that the other was in Ireland, but the panic induced by the news of Fitzmaurice's arrival with a Spanish expeditionary force was to have grave consequences for O'Healy and O'Rourke.

Shortly after their arrival at Smerwicke, the two Franciscans journeyed to the home of the Earl of Desmond in Askeaton, County Limerick. It was a relatively short trip to the banks of the river Shannon. They trusted Desmond, for he was a first cousin of James Fitzmaurice and his family had been implicated in counter-Crown activities. Askeaton was presumed to be a safe house for a

Catholic bishop, particularly one who was not anxious for the civil authorities to know of his whereabouts. The Earl was not at home when they called, but his wife Eleanor made them very welcome and entertained them for three days. The two Franciscans seem to have felt very relaxed there, for they freely divulged their plans to their hostess. They did not wait for the Earl's return but continued their journey through Limerick, O'Healy now en route to Mayo and O'Rourke heading home to Dromohaire.

A reception committee was waiting for them in Limerick. The Countess Eleanor had secretly notified the mayor of Limerick, a committed Tudor loyalist named James Gould, of the travel plans of the two Franciscans, an act of betrayal which provoked the following sexist comment from the bishop's biographer, Father Thomas Bourchier: "... he was received very graciously by the Earl's wife. But her outward show of kindness covered over her treachery, something that is common among women ..."

They were easily apprehended and quickly imprisoned in Kilmallock, about twenty miles south of Limerick. Only weeks after their capture and death, the Earl of Desmond was writing to the Tudor authorities, claiming the full credit for having had them arrested and interrogated. Both he and his wife were motivated by concern for their own predicament. Desmond's family had been associated with rebellion in the past and his cousin James' refusal to submit to the state religion was notorious. Sir William Drury, then Lord President of Munster, the most senior representative of the Crown in the district, was known to have doubts about Desmond's loyalty to the Queen. To be thought disloyal was to invite at best prosecution and possibly dispossession of one's lands. Desmond's ambivalence had made him vulnerable and he badly needed to protect himself and his family. His wife had presumably seen in the arrival of the Franciscans an ideal opportunity for her husband to demonstrate his loyalty once and for all. The priests were to be expended to protect the Desmonds. She may not however, have foreseen just how dire the consequences of betrayal were to be.

Lord Justice Drury felt himself to be oppressed on all sides. He was a career loyalist, transplanted to Ireland to do the Queen's work and to reap for himself as much in the way of money and property as he possibly could. Loyalism was an entrepreneurially sound business involving as it did the plundering of estates of recusant Catholics, but it was constantly hampered by the rebellious and recalcitrant Irish. The priests still refused to use the Book of Common prayer, the threat of open revolt was ever close to the surface, and now Fitzmaurice had landed with backing from the King of Spain. The Lord Justice's nerves were stretched to breaking point. He would be accountable to the Crown if things got out of control in his bailiwick. He was determined therefore, to suppress this new wave of disloyalty and he was prepared to go one step further than anyone had gone before. He was going to execute a Catholic bishop and that would put a stop to the pervasive sedition once and for all. However, he had a major problem. No jury trial of the two priests would produce a conviction for treason, or indeed of any offence which carried the death penalty. It was a criminal offence to refuse to take the Oath of Supremacy acknowledging Elizabeth as head of the Church, but only on a third conviction did the offence become one of treason. Drury had no evidence of any association between O'Healy and Fitzmaurice within the realm, something which was essential to found a charge of treason based on plotting against the Crown.

There was therefore, no trial. Instead, the two priests were taken to Limerick where they were subjected to a series of heavily biassed interrogations by Drury, acting under martial law. They were asked to acknowledge Elizabeth as Supreme Head of the Church, but both refused to do so, insisting that the Pope alone was head of the Church. The interrogation went beyond robust questioning. Bishop O'Healy was severely tortured. His fingers were severed from his hands by large spikes, but he remained strong in his assertion that his arrival in Ireland was unconnected to Fitzmaurice and that he had no role in any political action against the Queen. Drury offered to give him full recognition as Protestant Bishop of Mayo, with all the financial and social benefits which would follow naturally from such an appointment, if he would deny the Pope and the Roman Catholic Church. O'Healy replied that he would accept death rather than turn his back on his faith.

Drury was prosecutor, torturer, jury and judge. There was no opportunity to present a defence, and the Lord Justice pronounced the sentence of death by hanging. The two prisoners were bound hand and foot, set on horses and escorted by a platoon of soldiers to Kilmallock. O'Healy was fearless and unbowed according to bystanders whom he engaged in conversation along the twenty-mile route. The younger man was, however, distraught. O'Healy encouraged and exhorted him to welcome death and what lay beyond it.

Shortly before the hour of execution, Bishop O'Healy asked if he and Conn O'Rourke could be given permission to pray together. It was granted. Beneath the gallows they devoutly recited the litanies and then gave each other absolution. Conn O'Rourke was in danger of falling to pieces. O'Healy, despite his suffering, was in a state of deep serenity. His pity for the younger man was moving. 'Death', he told him 'seems to be a bitter breakfast but you will realise that there is a most pleasant breakfast in the future.'

The audience, some of whom had come to gawk, but many more to pray silently for the doomed Franciscans, fell silent as Patrick O'Healy prayerfully addressed the faithful among them. He begged them to value their faith and their fidelity to the Pope. He spoke emotionally about his vocation as a Franciscan and as a bishop, but before finally telling of the great joy with which he faced death for Christ's sake, he mentioned his persecutor, Lord Justice Drury, and warned him that his own days on earth were numbered.

He is said to have prophesied that Drury would die painfully and soon, and indeed seven weeks after the hanging Drury was dead from a sudden and frightful illness. A certain amount of wishful thinking and coincidence may well have distilled into an ex post facto presumption of the prophetic. Drury's death certainly provoked satisfaction in some quarters. The episode was recorded soon afterwards in the only native Irish record of O'Healy's martyrdom, the Annals of Loch Cé (pronounced 'key'), by the scribe, Brian MacDiannada of Moylurg, County Roscommon:

> "But God performed a plain, manifest miracle on the Justiciary; a burning attacked his head the day these two were hanged, and this burning did not leave him until he died of it in the course of a short time . . ."

O'Healy's biographer, Thomas Bourchier, wrote this the year after his death:

> "But God punished the judge who handed down the death sentence. The Viceroy took a very serious disease that he could not shake off. He died at Waterford... The Viceroy, acknowledging the hand of God in human affairs, agreed that the death of the bishop was the reason for his own terminal illness."

O'Healy's death was rapidly becoming a "cause célèbre"! Such assertions of divine vengeance visited upon the tormentor of the martyr are far from uncommon. Whether real or apocryphal, they added lustre and mystery to the martyr's story.

Bourchier's biography and the Annals of Lough Cé tell of O'Healy's exceptional holiness and in a country where political intrigue was widespread, the community was quick to identify

O'Healy and O'Rourke as martyrs for their faith and not for their politics, even though in the view of the English authorities, the two were coextensive. Four hundred people had been put to death by Drury in the decade and even the days before O'Healy was executed, but none was accorded the instant popular and widespread *fama martyrii* which erupted as news of the two Franciscans' deaths spread. The Catholic Irish were particularly outraged at the way the corpses were left dangling for several days on the end of the gibbets, to be taunted, mocked and violated by Crown supporters. But even then it seemed that if the plan was to belittle the two men, the opposite was the effect.

Bourchier describes the scene:

> "The bodies of the bishop and his companion remained on the gallows for a long time suspended by chains, but they did not change in any way in either appearance or colour. It looked as if they had only recently fallen asleep. A sweet scent exuded from the corpses so that crowds gathered to experience this. The people cut parts of the clothes off the sacred bodies and brought them home with them, so much so that the corpses hung there almost naked."
>
> ¶ "The town of Kilmallock was infested with large numbers of hounds and other dogs. Normally these would tear the bodies to pieces but in this case they left them intact. Birds did not bother about them either. It seemed that God was making the point that they were saints. . ."

Inevitably, as the first Irish bishop to die for the faith in Ireland, O'Healy became a legend. Over the centuries his story was told and retold in histories and martyrologies, never quite fading into oblivion. Four centuries later a new generation of Catholics re-examined his life and found a story worth retelling in an Ireland still trying to heal the legacy of the Reformation and Counter-Reformation.

CHAPTER 2

Matthew Lambert, Robert Meyler, Edward Cheevers and Patrick Cavanagh

All laymen, martyred 1581

They are

The deaths of the poor and ill-educated, even if ~~it is~~ by violent martyrdom, rarely make the contemporary headlines, never mind the history books. Thousands of Irish men, women and children died appalling deaths during the Elizabethan crusade to impose the Protestant faith on Ireland. Most were instantly forgotten, their lives and deaths unacknowledged and unrecorded, except perhaps in the bitter memories of their surviving family. History was a little kinder to the memory of Matthew Lambert, a poor baker, and his sailor companions, Patrick Cavanagh, Edward Cheevers, and Richard Meyler, though real life was unspeakably cruel to them. It is no accident that their names rise above the multitudes of forgotten ones. The special notice they have received was conferred on them by a case-hardened public over four hundred years ago. It was their own exact contemporaries, the people who knew them, worked with them and lived with them, who decided that these deaths were different from the litany of others, that these men were not just victims, but martyrs.

One day in the late spring or early summer of 1581, the quiet drudgery-filled lives of this small group of Wexford working men were irrevocably altered when the fugitive, James Eustace, Viscount

Baltinglass, stumbled across their paths. He was by then a pariah, hunted by the English forces and shunned by his peers. The kindly, pious Matthew Lambert offered him food and a bed, and the sailors helped him find a boat to take him to France. The first close encounter these impoverished men had with a member of the gentry cost them dearly. For their hospitality and kindness they were hanged, drawn and quartered.

The events which precipitated their deaths occurred in the east and southeast of Ireland, many miles distant from Limerick where the Fitzmaurice uprising was about to end in the defeat of the Catholic Irish. Just as the ill-fated crusade was disintegrating in the southwest, another champion of the Catholic faith, the Earl of Baltinglass, was deciding that he too had endured more than enough. Another uprising was about to begin, this time much closer to the English Crown's centre of authority in Ireland, in the area known as the Pale, the part of eastern Leinster with Dublin at its core.

The Pale is often simplistically characterised as a stronghold of loyalty to the Crown. The truth was much more complex. Many people gave willing political allegiance to the Queen, but spiritually their hearts often lay firmly with Rome. Catholic religious practice was well organised and reinforced by institutions like the trade guilds, where workers and tradespeople mixed their religious and secular interests to such an extent that the guilds formed an important bastion of Catholicism. Many of the leading gentry still openly practised their Catholic faith, and even among those who had converted to Protestantism there was a leitmotif of unwilling conformity. Their bodies appeared to conform, but their hearts and souls were elsewhere. The new Protestant faith was poorly explained to the people. Its enforcement was sometimes belligerent and sometimes careless, so that the Government's message on the subject was garbled and ambiguous. Mass was still openly celebrated, although it had been officially outlawed when the *Book of Common Prayer* was introduced during the reign of Edward VI. There was considerable resentment against the new form of worship. Some ignored it, others embraced it, and still more conformed outwardly, but seethed inwardly. The pot of discontent was already boiling when a further provocation was thrown in by a plan to levy taxes in order to pay for the Crown's army of occupation. Loyalty to the Queen was becoming a costly and intrusive business. The hapless people of the Pale, a fairly reactionary lot, were feeling the cold winds of change and having difficulty deciding what was for the best.

Typical of the dual thinking of the time was the situation of Gerald, the Earl of Kildare. His family, one of the leading Catholic families in the Pale, had its lands confiscated during Henry VIII's reign and subsequently restored during the brief reign of Henry's son, Edward VI. Edward was an ardent devotee of Protestantism. He was only ten years old when his father died and the succession passed to him as Henry's only legitimate son. Many of his subjects must have thought that with the coronation of a young and devout monarch, Protestantism had arrived to stay. One such was Gerald. Although educated in Italy by an uncle who was a Catholic cardinal, Gerald outwardly conformed to Protestantism, apparently because it was the safest thing to do. His sympathies were, however, secretly Catholic, though not sincere or strong enough to support any show of rebellion. He was an important and influential member of the gentry in the Pale, but having denied his faith in order to protect his family's inheritance, he was not about to jeopardise it all again. His wife was quite a different person. She was staunchly Catholic and openly entertained priests in her home, among them the Jesuit Robert Rochford, who was to be closely associated with the Baltinglass revolt. Her clear partisanship and her husband's ambivalence helped fuel the belief that the Earl would join with Baltinglass and bring a considerable amount of the Pale with him.

It did not happen. Gerald vacillated and eventually refused to participate, thus guaranteeing the failure of the revolt.

The Earl of Baltinglass was a man of unquestioned fidelity to the Catholic faith, although by background and social standing he was a member of the upper echelons of the Crown's most loyal subjects. Like Fitzmaurice, he had spent some time in Rome and had immersed himself in the Counter-Reformation. In July 1580, a year after Fitzmaurice landed at Smerwicke Haven in County Kerry, Baltinglass declared war on the Queen and her State Church. Although Fitzmaurice himself had been killed within four weeks of his arrival in Ireland, his poorly equipped little army had carried on under the new leadership of Sir John, brother of the Earl of Desmond whose wife had betrayed O'Healy and O'Rourke. Despite its lofty intention of promoting the Catholic Counter-Reformation, the Munster rebellion was soon reduced to a nasty squabble between two of Ireland's major clans, the Desmond Fitzgeralds and the Butlers of Ormond. The latter were the Queen's loyal henchmen and they did not miss their chance to finish off their old rivals, the Desmonds. The latter's vast estates were mercilessly conquered and the spoils divided among a group of people imported from England known as "Planters." These were devoted to their benefactor, the English Crown.

Baltinglass's war in the Pale fared no better. The absence of support from Gerald, Earl of Kildare, meant that help from the other leading gentry was not forthcoming either. They took their cue from the Earl and stayed resolutely on the sidelines. Baltinglass was forced to rely on some of the smaller, much less powerful families, in particular the O'Byrnes and the Cavanaghs, who lived in the mountainous area of County Wicklow south of Dublin. A ferocious struggle ensued in the mountains and at first Baltinglass met with some success. On 25th August he inflicted a massive defeat on the Government troops led by Lord Deputy Grey de Wilton.

The latter had failed to take due account of the strength of the O'Byrnes' grip on the area and his recklessness helped Baltinglass win a stunning victory at Glenmalure. The triumph, however, was to be very short-lived.

A few weeks later, in September, the long-awaited help from Spain sailed into Smerwicke. Full of enthusiasm, Baltinglass headed south to meet the Spaniards, hoping to join together the two sites of rebellion, Munster and Leinster. Before he could reach them, however, the Spanish troops were surrounded by Lord Grey and forced to surrender on 9 November 1580. In one of the most disgraceful episodes which litter this period, Grey ordered the massacre of all his prisoners.

Devastated, Baltinglass was now on the run for his own life, for clearly no one was to be spared. His troops were reduced to a handful and he toyed with the idea of surrendering himself, for there was precious little refuge. During these next haunted months, he was to find that he had few friends and fewer hiding places. His rich and influential acquaintances would in all likelihood have betrayed him in a minute. It became obvious that his only guarantee of safety lay in getting out of Ireland altogether. His companion during these days and weeks of frightening uncertainty was a Jesuit from the town of Wexford, Father Robert Rochford.

Rochford's hometown was a busy port and an "island of Englishry," according to the historian Patrick Corish. It had been the first part of Ireland to be settled by the Normans when they landed in the twelfth century, and since that time the English language and culture had apparently been absorbed easily into the social and political landscape. It is one of the ironies of this group of martyrs that Lambert, Cheevers and Meyler are all Norman names. Only Cavanagh is native Gaelic.

The English authorities believed that Wexford was loyal to the Crown, and on the face of it they had every reason to do so. In the regular attempts by the Gaelic sept, the Cavanaghs, to assert its authority over the town and county of Wexford, the town remained intractably pro-English. The imposition of Protestantism, however, provoked a crisis of split loyalties, just as it had in the Pale and elsewhere. As long as the Reformation changes were not enforced, life in Wexford continued as before, but once the *Book of Common Prayer* began to have an impact on worship, resentment increased. Wexford soon developed its own cadre of Counter-Reformation activists who grew in determination to resist the Protestantising of Ireland. They were mainly people of education and position in the town, merchants and shippers who had much to lose by their recusancy but who nonetheless remained firm in their fidelity to the Catholic Church. Through them, the port of Wexford was regularly used for the exchanging of information and intrigue between Ireland and Continental Europe. Fitzmaurice had used Wexford as a conduit to the mainland of Europe for years and had received help from local merchants who were broadly sympathetic to his cause. Many of the Anglo-Irish gentry, too, shared that same uneasy spirit of discontent and conflicting loyalties.

The two fugitives, Baltinglass and Rochford, had very few options open to them. There was no prospect of escape through Dublin. To head north at all was hazardous in the extreme. Wexford seemed to be their only real hope, given its sympathies and the fact that the route to it lay through land dominated by the Cavanaghs, who were supporters of Baltinglass. Rochford and the Viscount headed there in desperation.

But events had hardened Wexford hearts. Baltinglass was now an acknowledged failure, a wanted man capable of bringing disaster to anyone who assisted him. Every day those suspected of aiding him were being summarily executed. Some of the very substantial Wexford gentry, who had openly supported Baltinglass's revolt, were now paying a very dear price. A few of them were already in prison awaiting trial on serious charges. The rest were cowed into subservience. There was no chance they would risk their properties or their lives to save Baltinglass. They had too much to lose. The fugitives found the doors of the rich firmly shut to them. They turned to those who had nothing to lose but their lives, the pious, illiterate poor. Their immediate need was for food and a place to hide while they tried to obtain a safe passage to France. How they encountered Matthew Lambert is not known, but in his home their weary bodies rested a few hours.

Matthew Lambert owned a small bakery in the town of Wexford. It was a modest undertaking by all accounts, certainly not grand enough to justify an entry in the surviving town records which list the townsfolk of substance. Matthew Lambert is not among them. He was an unlettered man, as he described himself, but a very devout, prayerful Catholic, educated in the Faith like so many others by a mother of great piety. His mother's memory and her faith were dear to him and in his own gentle, simple way he was to show a physical and spiritual courage which would put his gentrified masters to shame.

Normally, his days slid one into the other in a daze of hard and unchanging labour, producing loaves for the townsfolk. The talk was all about political ferment and the failed rising. He, like others, must have hoped that the fallout would pass him by. But it was not to be. His predictable day's routine was interrupted by the arrival of Baltinglass and Rochford desperately seeking a night's shelter and food. Lambert was a soft-hearted, generous man, but he was no fool. He made his decision. He invited the two refugees into his home, knowing that in so doing he was risking execution. It was a momentous decision, but one which was taken willingly by this humble man. In his home he had learnt to respect priests and to show them hospitality. He would have seen it as sinful to refuse help to Rochford, and as for Baltinglass, a member of the Catholic aristocracy, he would have felt it a privilege to play a part in his escape. His great faith was stronger than his natural fear of the consequences. Despite his lack of formal education, Lambert had seen and heard enough to know that the assistance he was offering to the escapees was regarded by the authorities as treason. He knew the consequences, and he feared them just as much as the wealthy who had said no to Baltinglass, but he put his fears for himself aside and submitted to a course of action which he knew might end badly.

Five more poor men were to offer help. They were all sailors, but only three of their names have survived the vagaries of public and private records: Robert Meyler, Edward Cheevers and Patrick Cavanagh. Like Lambert, they were put on the spot by the appearance of Baltinglass in Wexford. They could have said no when asked to help, but they did not, even though summary executions of Baltinglass's supporters were taking place daily in other parts of the country. Instead, they tried to locate a boat to take the two men to France. Possibly they were betrayed, for the atmosphere of the times was thick with intrigue and distrust. Whether by betrayal or simply bad luck they were captured, although Baltinglass and Rochford fortuitously escaped and did eventually succeed in reaching safety abroad. Rochford's passionate involvement in the Counter-Reformation continued. Seven years later, in May 1588, he set sail from the Portuguese capital of Lisbon, bound for England with the doomed Spanish Armada. He was not among the survivors.

While Baltinglass and Rochford fled yet again, their erstwhile helpers were imprisoned, probably in the royal castle in Wexford. Unlike many other parts of the island where martial law was the norm, the ordinary common law courts were still functioning in Wexford so that jury trials were the standard mechanism for the determination of guilt or innocence. Whether their outcomes were any more just than under martial law is a matter of debate, but whatever the mode of trial, Matthew Lambert and his co-accused were not likely to benefit.

Jurors faced with defendants from the local landed gentry were loath to return verdicts of guilty against men on whom they might depend for their livelihood, and there had been several celebrated acquittals which had enraged the Crown officials. The most notable was the acquittal of Sir Nicholas Devereux, the head of the leading Anglo-Irish family in the area. He had openly admitted the "disloyal" conduct of which he was accused, but the jury was not minded to convict so notable a local dignitary. His acquittal outraged Lord Deputy Grey as he showed in the following extract from his letter to the English Privy Council dated 10 July 1581:

> ". . . and finding that some of the principale gentlemen of that county of Wexford had confederated with the rebells, and namely the best of the whole shier Nicolas Deverox, who had publiquely confessed before mee, and the whole assembly, matter worthy of death, I caused him to be arreigned, and although the most parte of the jury heard his confession and the matter so plaine and evidente as that it could not be denied, yet soche was theire unsounde dealing as they did most affectedlye acquite him, a plaine evidence to me how corruptly all causes for the queene are handled in the absence of the governour when in my presence so great an abuse was offredd . . ."

Still, someone had to deal with the Tudor wrath, and the deaths of poor, propertyless men might be enough to staunch the seething anger of the Crown officials. It was the misfortune of Lambert, Cavanagh, Cheevers and Meyler to be awaiting trial in such an atmosphere. They were easy targets, made even easier by their frank admission of everything they had done to assist Baltinglass, and their strong defence of the Catholic Faith.

Their trial was at one level a pathetic affair, these men of no rank and no education pitted against the scathing tongue of Her Majesty's judiciary. But in another sense, their very simplicity gave the proceedings a certain dignity and gravitas. Lambert acted as spokesman for the others, and though there is evidence that he and the sailors were most likely tortured and that they came under enormous pressure from family and friends to recant, he never faltered in his account. He was asked the inevitable question, the one which was tormenting hearts and minds across Ireland, and which even the most erudite minds were having difficulty answering: To whom did he give his loyalty, to the Pope or the Queen?

Lambert replied that he was an unlettered man who understood nothing about politics. He acknowledged the Queen's authority and was loyal to her, but his faith in God and the Church was a different matter.

"I know only one thing. I am a Catholic and I believe whatever the Holy Mother Church believes." That was all there was to his life and his beliefs. He was a Catholic, pure and simple. He had acted as a Catholic and nothing else. He intended no disloyalty to Her Majesty. Yet these words which four hundred years later in 1990 were to impress the Congregation for the Causes of Saints as "a case of wisdom, inspired by the Holy Spirit, coming from the lips of little ones" had a markedly different effect on the Court. They were interpreted as an assertion of loyalty to the Pope, and by this very fact were deemed to be a profession of disloyalty to the Queen. The latter was treason. The baker and the sailors were thus traitors and were sentenced to be hanged, drawn and quartered.

On or about 5th July they were dragged to the place of execution, hanged by the neck, and while still alive they were disembowelled and their entrails burned before their eyes. They were decapitated and their bodies severed into four parts. The English continued to use this barbaric form of capital punishment until its abolition in 1870. Ironically, it was last passed by way of sentence (but not carried out) on two Irish Fenians, fighting for their country's freedom in 1867, some three hundred years after the martyrdom of Matthew Lambert and his brave friends.

Patrick Cavanagh, Edward Cheevers, Robert Meyler and Matthew Lambert went to their gory deaths with a dignity and forgiveness which made them legends in a land pockmarked end to end with unremembered barbarities. Somehow their names soared where others did not. They were unconnected, unknown, uneducated, but the sheer simplicity and strength of their faith evoked in those who lived through those turbulent days a sense of profound reverence and respect. It was as if their actions, and their frank acceptance of the consequences, stood as a stark reproach to the perceived moral weakness of the lettered rich. Before long, their story was being told and retold across Europe.

CHAPTER 3

Dermot O'Hurley

Archbishop of Cashel, martyred 1584

D ermot O'Hurley's title of Archbishop is deceptive. Unlike his fellow clerics among the martyrs, he did not choose the priesthood as a young man. In a curious way, it chose him at a rather unlikely time in his life, well into middle age and long since settled into an enviable career. He was a fifty-year-old layman and highly successful academic when he was offered and accepted the Archbishopric of Cashel in County Tipperary, the county of his birth. It was not a prize for good behaviour. He had been away from Ireland and all its troubles for two decades, twenty years living the genteel life of a scholar of law and philosophy. When he said "yes" to Pope Gregory's offer of Cashel, he knew only too well that he was accepting more than the priesthood. He was accepting the probability of ending his days much more precipitously than his sedate life as a university teacher was likely to bring about. Within three years of his appointment, and within only months of his return to Ireland, he was executed as a traitor to the English Crown.

Dermot O'Hurley was born in County Tipperary around 1580, right at the start of the decade which was to provoke vast changes in England and Ireland. The great Lutheran debate which was going on so briskly elsewhere in Europe had barely touched Ireland. What did touch it, at first gently and then fiercely, was the decision of Henry VIII to break with Rome. Dermot was just a little fellow of six when the Irish Parliament declared Henry head of the Church in Ireland. Outwardly life did not change very much immediately, but the ominous signs were gathering. Choices would soon have to be made about allegiances, and those choices would have very real consequences. Dermot's father William, was an agent of the Earl of Desmond, the head of one of the powerful Anglo-Irish earldoms.

The position of the Desmonds was complex in this newly-emerging world. They were not a native Irish family but rather of the Anglo-Irish aristocracy who, through intermarriage and settlement, had merged into the Irish landscape without quite ever fully assimilating. To many of them, the native Irish were still inferior wretches, while England symbolised superiority and sophistication. They identified strongly with the latter socially and culturally, but like so many of the Anglo-Irish, they were spiritually Catholics. The Reformation and Counter-Reformtion put the Desmonds in a predicament which they finally resolved by putting their faith before fidelity to the Crown. That choice was to cost them everything, for just as O'Hurley was returning to Ireland as Archbishop, the fifteenth Earl of Desmond was hiding out in the Kerry mountains, trying to avoid arrest for his role in the unsuccessful Desmond rebellion.

The young Dermot was still a teenager when he set off for the Continent as an undergraduate at the famous Franciscan University at Louvain in Belgium, a decision which in itself says a lot about the family's attitude to faith and politics. He loved the place and the work, and graduated with the degree of Master of Arts at the age of twenty-one. Strongly attracted to the academic life, he joined the staff at Louvain and eight years later, as a recognised authority on Aristotle, he became Professor of Philosophy. Teaching and scholarship were his life. He took a deep interest in law also, immersing himself in relentless study to obtain the degree of Doctor of both Civil and Canon Law. His successful career in Philosophy gave way to a new career as dean of the Law School at Louvain and later Professor of Law at Rheims. Twenty pleasant years passed, during which he never returned to Ireland. His future seemed set in concrete, as a bookish unmarried don devoted to the pursuit of knowledge. He left Rheims, probably in 1570, and moved to Rome, presumably to take up another teaching appointment there.

Surprisingly little is known about his life in Rome from 1570 until his appointment to Cashel in 1581, but there is some evidence that he continued to work as an academic and scholar. That he was an outstanding Catholic layman who was highly regarded by the ecclesiastical authorities in Rome may be judged from the fact that he, who was not a priest, and had arrived at middle age without showing any inclination to become one, was offered the Archbishopric of Cashel. The Pope was unlikely to have made such an appointment without strong advice and support from the Curia, so it seems feasible to surmise that the reputation O'Hurley earned as an intellectual and profoundly spiritual man, in Louvain and Rheims, grew steadily during his years in Rome. Presumably his contribution to the contemporary politico/religious debates had marked him out as a man of strong and doctrinally sound views. What we do not know is how much of a surprise it was to him to be asked if he would like to be an archbishop, nor do we know how long he deliberated. Given the tranquillity of his life to date, however, it seems most unlikely that this major change came about as the result of a sudden rush of blood to the head of either O'Hurley or the Pope. More likely, it was the result of protracted debate and discussion about the politico/religious foment in Ireland, but once the decision was made, events began to move along quickly.

Having resisted the call to the priesthood for such a long period, O'Hurley rapidly made up for lost time by being propelled through tonsure, the four minor orders, the subdiaconate, the diaconate and ordination in sixteen days. This "fast-track" procedure required a special papal brief, which was issued on 15 July 1581. The archival records of the diocese of Rome show that Dermot O'Hurley spent the next two weeks in a frenzy of activity.

On Saturday, 29th July he attended the church of San Silvestro to be tonsured by the English bishop of St. Asaph, Thomas Goldwell. Bishop Goldwell eventually took him through all the stages of admission to the priesthood, including ordination.

The next day, both were back at San Silvestro for O'Hurley's admission to three of the four minor orders; the fourth was conferred two days later on 1st August, the Feast of St. Peter in Chains. The subdiaconate and diaconate followed on 6th August and 10th, respectively. On Sunday, 13th August he was ordained a priest at the church of the English College of St. Thomas of Canterbury in Rome.

Now that he was ordained, the Vatican appointed him formally to Cashel. A secret consistory was held on 11th September at the home of Luigi, Cardinal d'Este on the Quirinal, its purpose to authorise the provision of Dermot O'Hurley to Cashel as Archbishop. A second secret consistory held on 27th November completed the formalities by granting him the pallium, that is the woollen vestment conferred by the Pope on archbishops as a symbol of their investiture with high ecclesiastical office. The whirlwind process was now complete. Cashel had a new archbishop. His very existence was a recipe for conflict, for back in Ireland there was another Archbishop of Cashel, appointed in 1571 by Queen Elizabeth, a man with a very chequered past, Miler Magrath.

Magrath started out his clerical life as a Franciscan priest and had the distinction of being appointed Bishop of Down and Conor by the Pope in 1565. When the going got tough he changed sides, converting to Protestantism. His conformity was rewarded when Elizabeth appointed him to Cashel, though for the fifty years he spent there no one was entirely sure just where his allegiance lay.

After ten years of very half-hearted efforts to impose the new faith, and having endured accusations of being a covert supporter of the Mass, Magrath was shocked to discover that the Vatican had decided to appoint its own man to Cashel. At the time, appointments to Catholic bishoprics were in almost total disarray. The laws of the land made it virtually impossible for any appointee to take up his see without being arrested for treachery. Appointments were therefore not only sporadic, but were generally regarded as matters of considerable import.

The sudden spurt of energy which the Vatican exercised in ordaining O'Hurley was presumably for a purpose. It can surely not be a coincidence that he was appointed just as the Earl of Desmond's campaign against the Protestant monarch was about to disintegrate. With it went the entire power base of one of the Catholic Church's most important allies in Ireland. The fact that O'Hurley was a close acquaintance of the Desmond family lends considerable credence to the view that his appointment was designed to be a vital showpiece of Vatican support for the Counter-Reformation in Ireland. In fact, the Pope entrusted O'Hurley with a letter of support to the Earl of Desmond as well as verbal messages which the pope said he hoped "would be of great benefit and merit to you. Give all credence to these words." The Vatican would have been under considerable pressure to assist Desmond, so it is likely that consideration had been going on for some time about the most practical and feasible ways to show that support.

O'Hurley's personal reasons for wanting the appointment must also have been strongly influenced by the adverse fortunes afflicting his own family back home. Their once comfortable lifestyle in the shadow of the wealthy Desmonds was in ruins. It is thought that an older brother, William, got into enough serious trouble to receive a royal pardon in 1581, and his only sister, Honora, was destitute by the time her clerical brother was reunited with her in 1583. A younger brother, Andrew, was in the service of the Spanish military and probably not in a position to help. Dermot O'Hurley must at times have felt an overwhelming sense of frustration and helplessness as he heard of the bloody events in Munster which were overwhelming his loved ones and seemed to bode ill for his beloved Faith. Perhaps the contrast with his own comfortable world reproached him and provoked him to action. Whatever the reasons for the former law professor's fast track promotion, he did not, as one might expect, set out immediately for Ireland. Two years were to pass before his feet touched Tipperary soil again.

The new archbishop had a lot of groundwork to do before he could return to Ireland. Most of it he did at Rheims, to which he returned sometime in 1582. The memoirs of William Cardinal Allen show that O'Hurley arrived at Rheims with much needed cash for Dr Allen's seminary, a gift from the English College in Rome. They also indicate that the new archbishop became very ill while in Rheims, a fact which may explain his delay in reaching Ireland.

O'Hurley finally set sail for Ireland in the latter half of 1583, from the port of Le Croisic, at the mouth of the Loire. It was a quiet port and offered a degree of privacy not guaranteed elsewhere. His destination in Ireland was similarly discreet, the beach at Holmpatrick near Skerries, a small port just north of Dublin where it was hoped that the archbishop would be able to disembark like a phantom. A fairly forlorn hope, as it turned out.

O'Hurley was anxious to ensure not only his own safety but the safety of the papal documents which he needed as evidence of the validity of his consecration as archbishop. He decided not to carry them with him, entrusting them instead to the care of a merchant who was sailing back to Wexford. Unfortunately, the ship bound for Wexford was attacked by pirates and the documents were captured. Their importance was immediately obvious and with impressive speed they were handed over to the authorities in Dublin

Castle, presumably for a price. O'Hurley's precautions were set at nought. "The enemy" knew of his plans before he had even caught a glimpse of the Irish shoreline. Worse still, in the prevailing atmosphere of insurrection, espionage and counter-espionage, the news that the Pope was sending a new archbishop to Cashel, particularly one with a close family tie to the Desmonds, put the Dublin authorities into a state of hysteria. By the time O'Hurley reached Ireland, the word was out among the networks of pro-English spies to look out for a new and dangerous arrival. Good money would be paid for information telling of his whereabouts.

O'Hurley himself was of course totally unaware of this turn of events. He disembarked with some sense of foreboding, but his doubts and suspicions were allayed by a relatively trouble-free meeting with the Jesuit Father John Dillon on Holmpatrick beach. The two set off for the nearby town of Drogheda where they stayed too openly in a lodging house. Word of their location was immediately on its way to Dublin. Acting on a tip, they left hurriedly and headed inland to Slane Castle, home of Father Dillon's first cousin, the baron of Slane, Thomas Fleming.

Slane is only a few miles up the Boyne valley from Drogheda so the journey was a very short one. They were greeted at the castle with courtesy and hospitality, but O'Hurley was hidden in the castle's secret room and throughout his stay he used a pseudonym and did not disclose his clerical status to visitors. Little by little though the two men ventured out, making a number of journeys and returning safely to the castle. They made contact in Cavan with a number of priests who had been friends of O'Hurley's in his days as a lecturer at Louvain, Rheims and Rome, all popular centres of study for Irish clerical students at the time. The arduous journey to Cavan passed off uneventfully, and on their return to Slane the two clerics began to relax.

Among those to whom the archbishop disclosed his true identity at Slane was Piers Butler, of Duiske, the eldest illegitimate son

of the Earl of Ormond. The earl had a dozen or so illegitimate off-
spring but none were as favoured as Piers and none had the cachet
of being rumoured, as he was, to be the son of the earl's cousin,
Queen Elizabeth herself.

Thomas Butler, the Earl of Ormond and Piers' father, was a
legendary character. He adjusted his religious affiliation to the
prevailing monarch and so had professed both Protestantism and
Catholicism depending on which was in favour at any particular
moment. With his cousin Elizabeth firmly installed, Ormond embraced Protestantism, though his most profound commitment was
to the Butler fortunes and their preservation, at all costs.

The Ormonds and the Desmonds were old enemies despite
their common origins and a degree of intermarriage between them.
Now that Desmond was on the verge of capture with all the inevitably dreadful consequences for his followers, family and fortune,
Butler found it impossible to resist being part of the final deci-
mation of his rivals. He accepted an appointment as Governor of
Munster with the charge to suppress, as quickly and decisively as
possible, the Desmond rebellion.

O'Hurley was hopeful that through Piers Butler he might be
able to make direct contact with the earl, his father, in order to
plead with Ormond to spare the life of Garrett, the fugitive Earl
of Desmond, and to seek Ormond's protection for himself. Piers
agreed to take him to the Ormond home in Carrick-on-Suir, a considerable distance away and a journey undertaken more urgently
than O'Hurley would have liked.

The ramifications of skewed family loyalties, typical of the era,
were shown by the respective roles of the two Dillon brothers in
O'Hurley's few short weeks in Ireland. John Dillon, the Jesuit, ex-
posed himself to great danger by meeting the homecoming archbishop and travelling secretly with him from safe house to safe
house. His brother, Sir Robert Dillon, was an eminent Crown

ınd Chief Justice. He too visited Slane castle and was en-
ıed to dinner during O'Hurley's stay, though he was clear-
 ɔt trusted and was not taken into his brother's or O'Hurley's
confidence. Whatever disguise O'Hurley was using, Sir Robert was
not fooled by it. Over the dinner table the conversation, possibly
lubricated by fine wines, turned to legal matters. The former law
professor, well used to intellectual, legal discourse, participated too
enthusiastically in the discussion. His erudition alerted the vigilant
Sir Robert. Before he left the castle, he knew his fellow guest was
Archbishop O'Hurley. He also knew that anyone associated with
the archbishop was likely to attract very unhappy attention from
the authorities. The people most likely to suffer from that attention
were his own brother and his cousin, Thomas Fleming. Sir Robert
did not suffer from an overdose of fraternal scruples but went
straight to Dublin Castle and reported O'Hurley's whereabouts.

The archbishop, however, had noted Sir Robert's reaction. No
sooner had the Chief Justice departed than O'Hurley did the same,
realising that Robert's interest in his identity was not just for benign reasons. He left with Piers Butler for the Earl of Ormond's
fortress town of Carrick-on-Suir, over a hundred miles away but in
the heart of the archbishop's native county, Tipperary. From there
it was a stone's throw to Cashel. If Ormond backed him there was
still a chance his mission might succeed.

Initially the earl appeared to be willing to help, sending food
and drink to O'Hurley's lodgings and agreeing to meet the archbishop to discuss his situation.

The two men met, and while Ormond seemed to be genuinely
impressed by Dermnot O'Hurley and promised to give whatever
protection he could to the archbishop, he adamantly refused to
help the Earl of Desmond.

O'Hurley was naturally disappointed that he had not been
able to secure any degree of comfort for Desmond, but he took

Maid

Anatomy of a Scandal

(Michael Ebert)

1392
1954

3346
2397

5743

977
1954

— cue Messie
— Dark
— report
— check with ...

Ormond's offer of help to be genuine. He felt sufficiently reassured to keep a promise he had made to himself many months earlier when he was oppressed by almost insuperable obstacles. He had promised that if he were spared and arrived safely in Ireland, he would make a pilgrimage to the Abbey at Holy Cross where a relic of the true Cross was venerated.

The abbey's lands had, like much Catholic Church property of the era, been forcibly taken from Church ownership. They were now in the hands of the Earl of Ormond who turned a blind eye to the continuance of Catholic services at the abbey so long as it did not bring him into conflict with the authorities. O'Hurley made the short journey to Holy Cross which lies between Cashel and Thurles. He travelled not as the returning archbishop entering his diocese but simply as an ordinary pilgrim, his identity unknown. His journey took him close to the town of Cashel, and as he rode past he must have wondered if he would ever reside there as archbishop. What he did at the abbey is not known. He simply notes that he made the visit. One school of thought believes he did nothing more than attend Mass and pray like every other visitor. On the other hand, there is also a suggestion that his arrival was expected by the Catholics of Tipperary and that his visit to Holy Cross may have been his first public, albeit discreet, celebration as Archbishop of Cashel. If it was, it was not only his first, it was also his last.

There is some evidence too that he may have quietly paid a visit to his family, in particular his sister, or at least made enough contact with them to be very well informed about their circumstances, which were not good. Back in Carrick-on-Suir, his pilgrimage over and the immediate future looking a little less bleak now that Ormond seemed willing to support him, O'Hurley turned his thoughts to the completion of his mission. Sooner or later he was going to have to begin the process of ministering to his diocese. He was very anxious to avoid a confrontation with Miler Magrath, preferring instead to reassure the incumbent archbishop that his mission was purely and unambiguously spiritual and that he had no ambition to dislodge Magrath or challenge his authority. He knew that word of his arrival would greatly alarm Magrath and so O'Hurley wrote to him on 20th September intending to put him at his ease. The letter is by any standards deferential, for the archbishop makes much ado about Magrath's kindness to Honora O'Hurley, Dermot's impoverished sister. It is also the only letter written by O'Hurley to anyone which has managed to survive.

"If times would allow it, Most reverend Lord, I would come nearer so as to thank Your Lordship for the generosity you have shown to my sister, showing her every favour whenever opportunity required it. Indeed she herself informed me of this and I have learned it from others as well. For this reason I affirm that I am naturally obliged to reciprocate. For although S (i.e. my sister) consulted F (i.e. Dr Ambrose Forth, a master in Chancery) regarding the petition for inheritance, insofar as she was destitute of all help, I regard it as if done to myself."

Clearly, O'Hurley wished to appease Magrath and to get off on a sound footing with him. There is no hint of immodesty or triumphalism, nothing to churn up sectarian sediment or territorial fears. If O'Hurley felt personally at risk, there is no sign of it, but perhaps he would not have wished to display the remotest weakness before a man, whom at heart O'Hurley believed to be something of a moral dilettante.

But even as the letter was being written and the new archbishop was thoughtfully measuring every move he was to make, his caution was already thoroughly undermined by events in Dublin.

The Lord Justices in Dublin by now were fully conversant with everything O'Hurley had done and everyone he had seen since he arrived in Ireland. Thanks to Sir Robert Dillon they were aware that the Baron of Slane had hidden and entertained the archbishop, hospitality which in their view was tantamount to treachery. Slane was summoned to Dublin to answer accusations made against him by Dillon that he had knowingly harboured a priest and had failed to apprehend him.

Slane angrily retorted that he had no idea of O'Hurley's identity, but since Dillon had discovered it and was himself a Privy Councillor, why hadn't he arrested the archbishop when he had the perfect opportunity to do so at Slane castle? The Lord Justices saw in Slane's discomfiture a perfect opportunity to entrap the loathed archbishop. They turned up the pressure on Slane and offered him a deal: find O'Hurley and bring him to Dublin or face the full consequences of being found guilty of harbouring a priest. The harsh times made reluctant informers of the best of men. The Lord Justices were men of formidable cruelty and considerable power. Slane's liberty, his very life and his entire fortune were under threat. Sick at heart, he agreed to the deal and set out for Carrick-on-Suir to apprehend O'Hurley.

He had little difficulty finding the archbishop. He stopped off at Ormond's home and told him of the mess he was facing with the justices in Dublin. Ormond, the expert self-preservationist, was immediately anxious to put himself in a good light with the authorities by facilitating O'Hurley's capture. He directed Slane to the house in which O'Hurley was lodging. Slane arrived, not ostensibly as an arresting officer, but as a friend in distress. He recited all the things which had been said, done and threatened by the Crown agents. His association with O'Hurley was going to have the most dreadful consequences for his family, unless O'Hurley himself came to Dublin and helped exonerate the Baron. O'Hurley, dismayed to see the danger in which he had placed his friends, immediately volunteered to return to Dublin with Slane and explain to the authorities that the latter was innocent of any taint of wrongdoing. Even then, it seems O'Hurley did not foresee the critical situation he was now in, for before setting out for Dublin he asked the Earl of Ormond to deliver the letter he had written to Miler Magrath. The Earl took the letter, but for fear of appearing too closely connected to the archbishop who was now setting out for Dublin as a prisoner, he never handed the letter over to Magrath. There was no love lost between Ormond and Magrath, so it is possible, given the subsequent fate of O'Hurley, that Ormond's failure to pass on the letter was more than a wise precaution.

Dermot O'Hurley was put in chains, and the small party headed up the Kilkenny road to Dublin. During their overnight stops he was held in the local prisons, among them Kilkenny prison where word of his arrival provoked a less than timorous Catholic man to visit him. They talked about what lay ahead and the conversation turned to the reasonably fresh case of Peter Power, Bishop of Ferns, who had been so brutally tortured in Dublin Castle, shortly after his appointment in 1582, that he had given in and taken the oath of allegiance to the Queen. O'Hurley was very conscious of how easy it was to be strong when there was no real danger. During the conversation, he expressed his own deep fears about how he might handle himself in the same circumstances, knowing by now that they were very likely to face him in Dublin.

> "Many who are lions before the battle are timid stags when the hour of trial comes. Lest this prove true of me I pray to God for strength, for let him who thinks himself to stand take heed lest he fall."

It is one of the most curious ironies of the story of O'Hurley that these words ascribed to him also form part of the epitaph Miler Magrath chose for himself when he died many years later. He served half a century as Protestant Archbishop of Cashel and then, it is reputed, returned to the Catholic Church on his death bed.

Once in Dublin, both captive and captor were placed under arrest, O'Hurley in Dublin Castle and the Baron of Slane in better quarters, at the Lord Chancellor's in St. Sepulchre. The archbishop's interrogation began. It was clear from the outset that the Lord Justices were convinced he was deeply implicated in a papal plot to invade Ireland and overthrow the Queen's government. When after some twelve days of questioning they had been unable to elicit any information from O'Hurley to substantiate their fears, they wrote to the Queen's secretary, Sir Francis Walsingham, for advice.

His reply firmly instructed them to use "torture or any other severe manner of proceedings ... to gaine his knowledge of all forraigne practices against her Majesty States." This, directly from the Monarch, in spite of the fact that English Common Law expressly outlawed the use of torture. Lord Justice Wallop and Lord Justice Loftus wrote back suggesting that it would be better if O'Hurley was transferred to the Tower of London since Dublin Castle lacked sufficiently malign instruments of torture. The truth is that even the Lord Justices, who had a reputation for state-backed terrorism second to very few, were quite inhibited about torturing someone in so elevated a position as O'Hurley. It was not squeamishness which concerned them, but simple political intuition. They were afraid that if they tortured O'Hurley they might make the already disturbed political situation in the Pale worse rather than better.

However, Walsingham was exasperated by their reticence and their failure to get any useful information out of their prisoner. He retorted that they should first try gentle persuasion, but if that failed they were to "Toaste his feet against the Fyre with hot boots."

Boiling hot oil was poured into metal boots and the hapless O'Hurley forced to wear them over a fire. He revealed nothing, even in the face of appalling torments, for he had nothing to reveal. There was no conspiracy, no grand papal plan to attack Her Majesty's territories, just a simple gesture to the beleaguered

Catholic people that their spiritual welfare was of concern in Rome, such concern that they had at last appointed an archbishop of Cashel. He freely declared that he had been asked to carry letters to Ireland, but he had left these in France precisely because he wanted no truck with politics or violence. He openly admitted too that he had been present at meetings between Viscount Baltinglass and Cardinal Galli in Rome, but that there was no display whatever at these meetings of letters from Irish rebels, as was claimed by another man who had been present, the Crown spy, Christopher Barnewall. The latter's scaremongering and dubious testimony had fuelled fears of a massive Roman conspiracy in which O'Hurley was believed to be implicated. No amount of interrogation could uncover the existence of any such conspiracy or link O'Hurley to anything distinctly political. Even though Barnewall's story was doubted even by the authorities, they were nonetheless appalled at the idea of trained priests returning to Ireland to stiffen the faith and the resolve of the Irish people to resist the State religion. That was O'Hurley's central crime, to be an Archbishop of the Church of Rome and to be in Ireland.

The interrogation produced no evidence against the Baron of Slane and so he was released, but O'Hurley remained in jail. Now that he had been mercilessly tortured and his interrogations had yielded no evidence against him, the Lord Justices tried bribery. O'Hurley's suffering from the burns inflicted on him was dreadful. Thomas Jones, who was to become the Queen's Bishop of Meath, visited him in prison and tried to persuade him to submit to the Protestant faith. His poor sister Honora was also induced to visit him and try to tempt him with promises of high office in the State Church if he would turn away from the Catholic faith. He could not be tempted. His prayers for supernatural strength were it seems being answered. Where others had wavered under terrifying emotional and physical onslaughts, he did not.

The Lord Justices were at a loss to know how to proceed further. They had no confession, no evidence of any wrongdoing, and there was no prospect of O'Hurley submitting to the Oath of Supremacy. If he was tried before the ordinary courts it was very likely he would be acquitted, and neither they nor her Majesty could tolerate that. The only guarantee of a death sentence was to try him by a court martial. The matter was discussed by the Queen herself and the letter from her Chief Secretary Walsingham outlining her instructions make it crystal clear that O'Hurley was to be executed, preferably after a common law trial which would find him guilty of treason. But if that course of action might lead to his acquittal, then summary execution under martial law was permitted.

> "The man beyng so resolute as to reveal no more matter, it is thought meet to have no further tortures used agaynst him but that you proceade forthwith to his execution in maner aforesayd . . ."

The letter ends by reassuring the Lord Justices that their efforts with O'Hurley are very much appreciated by her Majesty.

The martial law decree of execution duly took place. There was no evidence, no semblance of a trial, and yet O'Hurley was sentenced to death. Surprisingly, the doomed archbishop seems to have retained some hope that Ormond might, even at this late stage, be able to come to his assistance. He wrote to him but the letter was intercepted and ended up like so much of the mail of the time, being redirected to the Lord Justices. A friend of Ormond's, Sir John Perrot, was shortly to take up the job of Lord Deputy, superseding the authority of the Lord Justices. The chances were that if O'Hurley's execution could be postponed until then, Perrot would be more merciful than Wallop and Loftus, the latter being incidentally also the Protestant Archbishop of Dublin.

The two Lord Justices took particular pleasure in designating Saturday 20th June 1584 as the day of O'Hurley's execution. Perrot took over on June 23rd. They wrote to Walsingham to bring him up to date on 9th July:

> ". . . and for our farewell two dayes before we delivered over the sworde beinge the 19th of the last (with the consent of the Lord deputie) we gave warrant to the knight Martiall in her Majesties name to do execucon upon him, which accordingly was performed, and thereby the Realme well ridde of a most pestilent member. . ."

It seems O'Hurley's death was all the sweeter to them because of its timing and they were delighted to be able to boast to the Chief Secretary that

> ". . . we have done but our dueties so we will not god willing at any time omitt to perform the same in lyke sort as occasion shelbe offered, especially in such matters as so highly concerne the glory of god and her majesties crowne and dignity, to whom we accompt we owe not only all our endeavours but also our lyves and our selves . . ."

God, it appears, was expected to be just as pleased with their day's work as her Majesty the Queen. Sadly for O'Hurley, as the letter shows, probably the first executive act performed by the incoming Lord Deputy was to give his consent to O'Hurley's execution, though the consent predated his formal takeover and may have been sought as much as a courtesy and a warning as for any legal effect it might have had.

The authorities had gone to some trouble to keep O'Hurley in close confinement in Dublin Castle so that news of his brutal treatment would not leak out and further disturb the peace. They wasted their time. While the archbishop was awaiting execution, his suffering was already a matter of scandal in Paris and Rome. Similarly, he was to be executed in the early hours of the morning so that there would be no one around to take any notice. As it happened, a group of men were practising archery close to the site of the execution at Hoggens Green, near the area of downtown Dublin now known as St. Stephen's Green. They looked on as this sad spectre made his way to the scaffold on legs which could only have borne his weight at the cost of considerable pain. O'Hurley was delighted to see them and begged the hangman for a couple of minutes to address them. He had the last word after all, delivered with great humility and patience, from the scaffold:

> "Gentlemen. First I thank my Lord and Saviour Jesus Christ because it hath pleased his divine providence to send you hither to bear testimony of my innocent death, being that it was meant I should dye obscurely. as may he seen by sending me to this place of execution so earely. Be it therefore known unto you (good Christians) that I am a priest anointed and also a Bishop, although unworthy of soe sacred dignities, and noe cause could they finde against me that might in the least degree deserve the paines of death, but merely for my funcion of priesthood wherein they proceeded against me in all pointes cruelly contrarie to their owne lawes, which doth priviledge any man that is worth ten pownd in goods not to dye by Martiall Law, which I leave between them and the Majesty of the Almighty and I doe injoin you. (Deere Christian

Bretheren) to manifest the same unto the world and also to bear witness at the day of judgement of my innocent death. which I indure for my function and profession of the holy Catholick Faith . . ."

He ended by asking them to join with him in prayer for his soul. The story of O'Hurley's death was carried like a contagion throughout Dublin. A group of pious and courageous Catholic women rescued his body and brought it to the little church of St Kevin in nearby Camden Street, where it was buried with great reverence and affection. The archbishop's clothes were kept as relics, and as the story of his violent death gathered momentum, his grave became a place of regular pilgrimage among the Catholic people. Reports of miracles ascribed to Dermot O'Hurley began to circulate and his fame as a martyr grew as written accounts of his death were published. These accounts were republished from time to time throughout the following three centuries. So well documented was his *fama martyrii* that when the cause of the Irish martyrs was being pleaded before the Congregation for the Causes of Saints, the title of the cause read simply, "Dermot O'Hurley, Archbishop and companions."

CHAPTER 4

Margaret Ball (Bermingham)

Laywoman, died a martyr in Dublin Castle, probably in 1584

Margaret Ball is the sole woman among the seventeen martyrs, and hers is probably the most extraordinary story of all. She bore twenty children, two of whom became Lord Mayors of Dublin, and it was Walter, the eldest and the most successful, who condemned his own mother to her pitiful, slow death in prison. Self-preservation, long a characteristic of the rich and influential, in this Ireland of torn loyalties, had never been a respecter of familial ties. Neighbour had betrayed neighbour, cousin had betrayed cousin, brother had betrayed brother, and now a son betrayed a mother, who forgave him to the end. A cynic might say that any woman who brings twenty children into the world is looking martyrdom in the face most days of the week, but Margaret Ball's pathetic death stands in stark contradiction to her very promising start in life as the well-to-do daughter of a country squire.

The precise date of Margaret's birth is not known, but it was probably sometime in 1515 that she was born into the Bermingham family of Corballis, in the Barony of Skyrne, County Meath. Her home was near the legendary Tara, seat of the High Kings of Ireland. It was a rural area about twenty-five miles from Dublin, but within the Pale. Her parents, Nicholas and Catherine Bermingham, were members of the gentry, so young Margaret enjoyed a sheltered life of comfort and privilege. She appears to have been very well-educated and to have received a strong spiritual formation. The family was a religious one and later, when all such families were forced to choose between Crown and Pope, the Berminghams became synonymous with opposition to the Tudor government's harsh enforcement of State Protestantism. But all that still loomed only vaguely in the future when Margaret danced and played her way through a trouble free childhood. She married in 1530 when she was still in her mid teens, though whether it was a love match or an alliance between a family with status and a family with money is not known. In any event, it guaranteed her a wealthy life and a prominent place among Dublin's best known and most influential citizenry. Her husband, Bartholomew Ball, was born in Balrothery in north County Dublin but raised in Dublin city from the age of seven. He was one of Dublin's most prominent and prosperous merchants. Given his status at the time of the marriage, it seems likely that he was considerably older than his wife. On their wedding day in 1530, Margaret and Bartholomew probably knew very little and cared even less about the controversy raging in England over Henry VIII's attempts to extricate himself from his marriage to Catherine of Aragon. Margaret was no more aware of the fact that she was entering a marriage which would ultimately cause her martyrdom than was Sir Thomas More, who as newly appointed Chancellor only a few months earlier had opened the English Parliament which was to decree his death.

Margaret and Bartholomew had twenty children, but in those days of high infant mortality only five survived into adulthood, Eleanor, Katherine, Nicholas, Thomas and the notorious Walter. Margaret herself seems to have come through these pregnancies relatively well. To have survived them at all showed a remarkable constitution, and it is sadly ironic that having struggled through a succession of pregnancies and infant deaths to what should have been a very placid old age, Margaret faced the most cruel challenges of her life long after her family was reared and enjoying success. She and her husband shared thirty-eight years of marriage, during which they were respected and powerful citizens of Dublin who took a very active role in the commercial and political life of the city. Bartholomew became both bailiff of Dublin in 1541, and later Mayor of the city in 1553. The political temperature rose steadily during those years and as it did Margaret's own family, the Berminghams, became deeply embroiled in the Pale's growing disenchantment with Tudor rule. Bartholomew died early in 1568 leaving the new Widow Ball well provided for. She could easily have faded from view, passing her days happily conforming to the new Protestantism, or at least not openly challenging it. But Margaret came from a family whose adherence to the Catholic Church never wavered. She had a streak of independence and a fearlessness which set her off down the path of recusancy, fully aware that she was pitting herself against the law of the land.

A William Bermingham, who was most likely Margaret's brother, was the leader of a delegation sent to London by the gentry of the Pale to complain about the harsh treatment being meted out by the Earl of Sussex's administration in Dublin. William's son, Patrick, who lived at Corballis in the barony of Skryne, where Margaret was born, was also in the forefront of resistance to state-backed repression. The name of Bermingham was not popular with the Crown officials. Their recusancy was deemed outrageous and all the more irksome because of their wealth and prominence. Margaret was a talented and energetic woman whose being revolved round an unshakable faith in God and a life filled with prayer. She loved young people and she loved her Faith, and she brought both together in a sincere desire to share her gift of Faith with the young people of the Pale who were being subjected to such mixed messages about Church, state and faith. Margaret's message was straightforward, the Mass was the centre, the core of her life and the Roman Catholic Faith was her road to God. Whatever the politicians might will or decree, she was determined to use her wealth and her intellectual and spiritual resources to fight them every inch of the way. The recusant families struggling to hold on to their Catholic faith were under enormous pressure inside the Pale. The temptation to conform to Protestantism dangled before them, promising security and access to continuing privilege. As the screws tightened and the penalties for failing to conform bit deeper and deeper, the faith and courage of the recusants was tested daily.

Margaret Ball felt keenly that those who, like herself, were determined to resist the encroachment of force-fed Protestantism needed to support each other in practical ways. She opened a school for the children of Catholic families and it soon became a popular centre of learning, as noted for its high level of scholarship as for the piety of its students. Children travelled long distances to Widow Ball's school drawn by her reputation for instilling virtue, spirituality, and fidelity to the teaching of the Catholic Church.

Where many of the gentry played down their recusancy, Margaret did not. Her school, which catered to the children of recusant families, operated openly. Priests on the run often used her home as a place of refuge. They were welcomed, given food and shelter, and allowed to celebrate Mass there, despite the grave penalties which such actions could bring down. Margaret's elevated status in the Pale provided virtually no immunity from prosecution and she had several skirmishes with the law, none of which intimidated her in the slightest. Sometime in the late 1570s, while a fugitive priest was saying Mass in her home, the house was raided and Margaret was arrested. Her good standing in the community was not sufficient to keep her out of jail and she spent a brief uncomfortable time there. Some of her friends among the nobility, by dint of pressure and the judicious application of money to the right people, managed to have her released.

The brief spell in prison did not inhibit Margaret. She continued as before, keeping an open door to priests. Her biggest disappointment in life was her eldest son, Walter. Most mothers would have been proud to have a son who followed his father into the office of Lord Mayor of Dublin, as Walter did in 1580. However, Walter converted to Protestantism and became a zealot. He was adamant that his mother was wrongheaded in her loyalty to Rome. Margaret was dismayed that her son had turned his back on the faith of his ancestors and embraced the state religion which his family had resisted at great personal cost. She never missed an opportunity to surround him with committed Catholics in the hope that he would join the recusants, among whom was his own younger brother, Nicholas. Nothing she tried had any effect. Walter remained as staunch a Protestant as she was a Catholic. Both of them were to have their respective faiths sorely tested.

It was the year 1580 and the Pale was a hotbed of Reformation and Counter-Reformation intrigue. The Baltinglass uprising had fuelled panic in the administration. There was a morbid fear that the Pale would erupt into a general, widespread rebellion. The atmosphere was combustible. The Crown was at loggerheads with the recusants who were seen as the primary focus of disobedience to the law. Increasingly they were seen as subversive and in need of control. There were two ways of controlling them. They could be persuaded to convert or they would be repressed. Families divided under pressure and those who embraced Protestantism had all the intensity and certainty of the recently converted. Some, like Margaret's eldest son, turned on their Catholic friends and relations.

Walter Ball, Mayor of the capital city and a much respected business man, had taken the momentous step of alienating himself from his family and their faith. He was now a fervent Protestant and a supporter of the Crown. From the moment of his conversion until his death, Walter never wavered in his wholehearted commitment to Protestantism and his seething aversion to Catholicism, which he regarded as little more than superstition. He embraced all the popular Protestant causes, becoming particularly associated with the movement to found a Protestant university in Dublin. When the University of Dublin (Trinity College) was founded in 1592, Walter was listed among its patrons and he received special congratulations from Queen Elizabeth for his contribution to the new university. When the new college opened its doors, Walter's two sons were among its first alumni. The stoutly Protestant ethos of the college continued well into the twentieth century, and although it lifted its ban on Catholic students, as late as the 1970s, Catholic students still had to ask permission from the Catholic Archbishop of Dublin to attend the "Protestant university." By the time Trinity College celebrated its four hundredth anniversary in 1992, its student body and its staff represented the entire Irish community and it was ironically being governed by a Catholic Provost. Perhaps had Walter been able to see that far ahead, he would have been less anxious to include in his will a substantial bequest to Trinity College for the maintenance of four scholars. As it was he was now embroiled, just about as deeply as it was possible to be, in the battle to make Ireland Protestant.

There were those among Walter's newfound conforming friends who were sceptical of the depth of his conversion. After all, just look at his family. His mother's front door was never closed to priests, who were criminals in the eyes of the law. She was among the most notoriously public recusants, and her son Walter's mayoralty, far from making her more circumspect in her support for the Counter-Reformation, seemed to have the opposite effect. Walter's younger brother Nicholas was no better. He too was a very well-known businessman in the Pale, yet he sided with his mother. Walter felt that his position was critical. He needed to prove to his newfound colleagues and to himself that he was truly a reformation man. The best way to do that was to make an example of his mother.

Walter had been appointed to the court of high commission, which investigated cases of alleged recusancy. It is not known for certain how Margaret fell foul of the authorities, but it is possible that she was asked to appear before the commission to answer charges of harbouring priests or facilitating the celebration of Mass. Because of her previous entanglement with the law, the court was unlikely to be merciful to her. There was a bitter war going on for hearts and minds and the schism in the Ball family was a potent symbol of what was happening throughout the community. With Walter's firm support behind them, the authorities were now in a powerful position to show just how much they meant business by strictly enforcing the law against one of the Pale's best known dissenters.

Margaret was taken from her home and dragged through the streets strapped to a contraption known as a hurdle, a wooden sled-like frame used to drag convicts to the gallows. She was imprisoned in Dublin Castle where conditions were squalid. This time there was no prospect of release. One can only imagine the internecine feuding which her imprisonment must have provoked between Nicholas and Walter, but the latter grew more resolute in his view that Margaret's fate was entirely her own fault and that she could easily redeem the situation by abandoning Catholicism.

The Widow Ball had never known poverty. She had never gone hungry or been forced to live without basic home comforts. Now in her late sixties, she was to spend her remaining years in conditions of appalling dirt and neglect. She prayed her way through it and through the squalor-induced illness, which took a heavy toll on her body, though not her spirit. She was not at all concerned about herself or anxious to obtain her freedom. Her sole anxiety was for her son Walter and his bitter opposition to the Catholic Church. She prayed constantly for his conversion.

The days and weeks became years, yet Margaret faced each dreary day with the same resilience. In 1582, her other son Nicholas became Mayor of Dublin, but there was virtually nothing he could do to save her. The case was too notorious for the authorities to simply change their minds. If Margaret was to be freed, then she would have to change her mind. Margaret knew well that the doors would open and her warm comfortable life of privilege would embrace her again if she would just surrender her Faith, but even as she grew physically weaker, ravaged by disease and hunger, she found strength to say no and to keep on saying it until the end.

Worn out by the misery of prison life, she finally died, probably sometime in 1584. Shortly after her death Nicholas became a member of Parliament and both he and Walter continued to prosper in their different spheres. Two wealthy, powerful and influential brothers, not at all the kind of men whose mother would be expected to die from the effects of malnutrition and hardship in a dank, damp prison cell. Hers was a slow tortuous martyrdom, a daily grinding down of the body in the hope that the mind and spirit would collapse too. But mother and son were cut from the same cloth. Neither gave in. Walter lived for his faith; his mother died for hers. The recusants of the Pale cherished her memory and from the moment of her death she was seen quite simply as a martyr whose deep, boundless love of God and her unflagging forgiveness soared above the hatred and sectarianism of the times, giving strength to those still fighting for the right to believe and worship as they chose.

CHAPTER 5

Father Maurice MacKenraghty

Martyred in Clonmel, County Tipperary, 20th April 1585

Maurice MacKenraghty was one of a number of martyrs whose fate was linked to Gerald, the fifteenth Earl of Desmond, but whereas Gerald's involvement in the capture of two of the earlier martyrs had been ignominious, this time his role was quite different. Gerald appears to have been transformed from an ultra-cautious man anxious to ingratiate himself with the authorities to an outright rebel, leading a doomed insurrection. In his earlier guise he had betrayed the two Franciscans, Bishop Patrick O'Healy and Father Conn O'Rourke, and boasted about how he had helped procure their deaths. Now as a dissident, he too faced death, and among the few who remained loyal to him was his friend and confessor, Father Maurice MacKenraghty.

Father Maurice was a Limerick man, born in Kilmallock, a fortress town in Desmond's territory. His date of birth is not known, nor is much information available about his education and training for the priesthood. Kilmallock was a wealthy centre of commerce and an attractive place for an ambitious tradesman to set up shop. Maurice's father, Thomas, came originally from Irraghticonnor in County Kerry, but he moved to Kilmallock to pursue his trade as a gold and silversmith. He was clearly an

ambitious man and the town offered prosperity and the patron-
age of the Desmonds. As the son of a successful businessman,
young Maurice grew up in a busy but comfortable household. He
was a quiet fellow, intense, devout and not given to saying much.
The political environment in which he lived, however, was always
verging on eruption, and the MacKenraghtys tied themselves to
the fortunes of their masters, the Desmonds.

In 1569 and again in 1579, the Earls of Desmond led upris-
ings against the Crown and the Reformation in Ireland. On each
occasion the province of Munster had been ravaged by four years
of vicious fighting. The Desmond territories were impoverished
and ruined. Maurice's father seems to have committed himself to
the Desmond cause, for in April 1566 and January 1570 he was
obliged to ask the Queen for pardon for his offences committed in
support of Desmond's uprising. He was luckier than his son, for his
requests for mercy were granted.

Gerald, the fifteenth Earl of Desmond, was a first cousin of
James Fitzmaurice Fitzgerald, charismatic leader of the unsuccessful papally backed revolt of 1579. When James was killed in battle on 18th August, only a month after arriving in Ireland with
his small army, it was Gerald's two brothers, John and James, who
took over leadership of the war. Gerald was differently inclined.
His actions indicate a man anxious to appease the Crown officials
rather than pit himself against them. Although his family name was
held in very high regard in Rome, his wife Eleanor had denounced
the trusting Bishop O'Healy and Father Conn O'Rourke to the
authorities. Her actions led directly to their arrest and execution.

Eight weeks after the deaths of the two Franciscans, Gerald
wrote a grovelling letter to Thomas Butler, the Earl of Ormond,
who was head of the Crown forces in Munster. It contained a litany of all the services performed by the loyal Gerald in further-
ance of the interests of the Crown. Clearly, Gerald was worried

about his standing with the authorities, so worried that he was prepared to exaggerate his involvement in the capture of O'Healy and O'Rourke in an effort to impress Ormond. He described his cousin James Fitzmaurice as the "Traitoure," no doubt to underline that he himself was a faithful servant of the Crown to the core and in no way associated with his rebel relations. The letter is dated the 10th of October 1579.

On 15 November 1579, barely five weeks later, the same Gerald captured and pillaged the town of Youghal, an act tantamount to a declaration of war against the government. In the eyes of the law Gerald himself was now "the Traitoure," hunted by his fellow peers Ormond and Fermoy, both of whom were related to him. The second of these, Viscount Fermoy, was a Catholic. To describe the times as confusing would be a gross understatement. Gerald's actions had at least the benefit of finally clarifying where the Desmonds stood. It was precisely where the Ormonds always suspected they stood, no matter how craven the letters from Gerald had been.

While Gerald was vacillating and throwing up a variety of smoke screens, Maurice MacKenraghty, his chaplain, was earnestly spreading word of the Counter-Reformation around Kilmallock. He was an energetic priest devoted to the pastoral needs of the people of the area, among them the local lord of the manor. It is not known if Father Maurice knew of the Earl's part in the martyrdom of O'Healy and O'Rourke. It seems unlikely that he did. Desmond was a master of duplicity and in any event there were very mixed views among the well-to-do about bringing another expensive and potentially disastrous war upon themselves.

Father MacKenraghty had no interest in fighting, but now that the Earl of Desmond was at war, he believed that his place, as chaplain, was to be with him, not as a rebel against the Crown, but as a bringer of the Gospel, whose ministry was needed more urgently on the battlefield than anywhere else. For the next four years he followed the Earl through the misfortunes of an ill-judged war that saw the rebel forces reduced to only ten by September 1583. On 17th September the little group was spotted by spies. They tried to flee but MacKenraghty was captured because, as his captor's report said, he "was not so well horsed as the rest." Gerald escaped only to be fatally wounded in an incident near Tralee, County Kerry, nine weeks later. The man responsible for MacKenraghty's capture was Maurice Roche, Viscount of Fermoy. He was a Catholic and a relative of both Gerald and the Earl of Ormond. There was more than a suspicion that Roche had deliberately let Gerald escape and then had exaggerated the importance of the priest in order to allay any suspicions about his commitment to routing Gerald. In that miasma of overt and covert loyalties and relationships, anything was possible.

The captured priest was taken to the prison in Clonmel with orders from Ormond that he was to be interrogated "by fayr or fowle means" so that he would open "the secretes of his hart."

Clonmel was an Ormond town, but like many county towns in Ireland it too was debating where it stood on the big contemporary issue, Queen or Pope. Life was becoming ever more complicated for the townsfolk. The long-established practice of the faith of their forefathers was now outlawed, their lord, Ormond, had embraced Protestantism but not with any obvious enthusiasm, and the future looked uncertain as wave after wave of disaffection broke out across the country. There was plenty of discreet Counter-Reformation activity, and among the clannish, well-to-do business folk there was a thriving, clandestine Catholic community. They had no regular priest to minister to them and depended on the occasional fugitive for Mass and the other sacraments. Through their extensive network of contacts they were able to get in touch with Maurice MacKenraghty in prison and so, although he passed eighteen long months there, he was able to exercise his priestly ministry to a limited extent, under the eyes and probably with the connivance of the prison authorities. The faithful Catholics of Clonmel felt the absence of Mass and confession very deeply. They were prepared to take any risk to be able to practise their faith, and as Easter of 1585 loomed, they decided on a dangerous course of action. A Clonmel merchant named Victor White bribed the senior jailer at Clonmel prison to obtain MacKenraghty's release for one night so that he and his family and friends could fulfil their religious Easter duties. The jailer was not hard to persuade and possibly at the time the deal was made it looked as if everyone concerned would comfortably get away with it. The priest spent the night of 10th April in White's home hearing confessions in preparation for the celebration of Mass on Easter Sunday. The timing turned out to be fatal. Sir John Norris, the President of Munster, arrived in the town. It was not the best moment for a well-known prisoner to be absent without leave from his cell. The jailer, realising his own neck was at risk, betrayed MacKenraghty's whereabouts. White's house was surrounded and attacked just as the secret, outlawed Mass was about to begin in front of a substantial congregation. The raiding soldiers provoked a melee. People fled, panic-stricken in all directions. Some jumped through windows, others attempted to hide in the basement. Father Maurice hid himself in a haystack. A soldier prodded it with a bayonet, wounding him in the thigh. He stifled his cries of pain and amazingly went unnoticed. When the raid was over, the altar lay in ruins, many of the faithful were wounded and arrested, but the priest had escaped.

Victor White was taken into custody and interrogated. His captors threatened to kill him unless he revealed MacKenraghty's hiding place, but he refused. When word reached MacKenraghty that White's life was in serious danger because of his reluctance to betray his friend, MacKenraghty decided to surrender. He sent a messenger to White telling him of his decision, but Victor White was adamant. He was fully prepared to die rather than sacrifice the life of the priest. He had known from the outset that the enterprise was fraught with mortal danger, and now that it had arrived on his doorstep he was not going to sidestep it. MacKenraghty, however, was just as determined. He came out of hiding and was soon back in Clonmel prison.

The incident was now a cause célèbre. With the integrity and courage shown by White and MacKenraghty stirring the recusants' blood, Sir John Norris badly needed to cut them down to size. He was not immediately keen to create another martyr whose death might further encourage the recusants. MacKenraghty was much more useful alive if he could be persuaded to embrace Protestantism. The impact on the frightened and confused recusant community would be devastating. It would emasculate the Counter-Reformationists and enhance the validity of the Protestant cause. Norris offered Father MacKenraghty a way out. Swear on oath that the Queen was the head of the Church, and not only would he be freed but he could name his own price. He could have anything he wanted if he would simply take the oath of supremacy, just a formula of words.

The priest quietly but persistently stated his belief in the Catholic Faith. He could not and would not accept the Queen of England as his spiritual leader. Norris ranted abuse, but his prisoner was unshakeable. Angry and exhausted, Norris sentenced him to death as a traitor - a sentence he is reported to have listened to with impressive serenity. Norris tried one last time to get him to renounce the Catholic Faith but nothing swayed him, not even the persuasive powers of a Protestant minister who visited him in prison and tried to cajole him into changing his mind. There is no doubt that it would have been a considerable publicity coup if Norris had been able to convert the priest, but there was no inducement or threat which could bring him to take the Oath of Supremacy. The sentence of death by hanging, drawing and quartering, imposed without trial, was ordered to be carried out.

On his way to the scaffold shortly after Easter, Father MacKenraghty asked to make the last part of the journey on his knees. He was calm and happy making his own slow Way of the Cross, although the route was lined with jeering mobs. He arrived at the site of the execution, then turned and preached a short homily to the crowd. There was no anger or bitterness, no call for retaliation. He asked them to hold fast to their faith in God and in the Catholic Church and to remember him in their prayers. They were moved to tears by his humility. He blessed them and mounted the gallows showing no fear.

The noose tightened around his neck and he dropped downwards, dangling but still alive from the end of the rope. The soldiers grabbed his body and beheaded it. In accordance with the sentence, the body was to be quartered, but some of the Catholics present are believed to have bribed the executioner to leave it alone. Father Maurice's head was displayed in public for the next few days until his body was bought by local Catholics and buried quietly behind the high altar in the church of the nearby Franciscan friary, which like most of the monasteries of the time had been closed by Government decree.

From the moment he died, Maurice MacKenraghty was revered in Clonmel as a martyr. The area in which Victor White lived became known as Martyrs Lane, and the legend of martyrdom coloured local folk history for generations.

Why anyone would embrace the priesthood in Ireland in those days defies explanation. Priests were treated as outlaws at best, and traitors at worst. Every day they spent in Ireland they risked discovery, imprisonment, torture and death. Simply to eat and sleep they had to place enormous trust in friends, family and strangers, who might at any moment betray them. Their heads, cut from their bodies, were hoisted aloft in town squares to ensure that other young men would get a clear message that the priesthood was not good for their health. Remarkably, the town and district of Clonmel experienced a surge in the number of vocations to the priesthood in the wake of Maurice MacKenraghty's death.

CHAPTER 6

Dominic Collins

Jesuit Lay brother, martyred in Youghal,
County Cork, 31st October 1602

D ominic Collins was thirty-six years old when he was hanged in Youghal, County Cork, the town of his birth. He had not been home for over fifteen years, and this was his first visit since he had set out on a life of adventure as a headstrong twenty-year-old. It was the tragic finale of a colourfully chaotic career.

Youghal was a bustling port and an administrative centre for the Crown when Dominic was a lad. His family were evidently important citizens, for both his father and brother became mayors of the town. The practice of the Catholic faith in the area went up and down depending on whether soldiers were garrisoned in Youghal. The military base was not permanently manned, but from time to time a company of soldiers would be deployed there. When the soldiers were in town, the priest quietly departed. When the soldiers moved on, the priests moved back in. Among the priests who ministered in Youghal during Dominic's childhood was the Wexford Jesuit, Robert Rochford, who later joined the Earl of Baltinglass in trying to leave Ireland, an attempt that caused the martyrdom of the four Wexford martyrs, Matthew Lambert, Patrick Cavanagh, Edward Cheevers and Robert Meyler.

It is not known if young Dominic attended the school which Rochford opened in Youghal, but given his fascination with the Jesuits when he grew to adulthood, it is possible that he did. The school did not operate for very long. The upheaval wrought in Youghal by Gerald, Earl of Desmond in November 1579, set off a chain of events which forced the Jesuit school to close and ended Robert Rochford's career as a teacher.

Youghal was within Desmond territory but its political temper favoured the Crown, though like everywhere else in the country it was adjusting very unhappily to the enforcement of the new State religion. Still, life was not as difficult for Catholics in Youghal as it was in the Pale, for Protestantism was imposed here with less rigour. The citizens of Youghal were willing enough to live with the haphazard demands of the Crown and had adopted a workable, if duplicitous *modus vivendi*. They were not particularly willing to risk their prosperity and peace by siding with the Fitzmaurice or Desmond rebellions. When Gerald finally stopped vacillating and threw his lot in with the rebels, Youghal did not support him. If its people thought that they were going to be allowed to sit out this conflict quietly, they were badly wrong, for Youghal was the first town to feel the brunt of Gerald's rage. It was the start of a period of terror and destruction. The fortified walls of the town were pulled down, and the property of loyalists was sacked and looted. The townspeople fled as Government forces fought with Desmond's troops to control the town. When the Earl of Ormond arrived in another effort to free the town, he found an empty shell, deserted and in ruins.

The busy, once wealthy port, which had boasted a sophisticated infrastructure, was left with only rubble and a long hard struggle to find its way back to peace and prosperity. In these troubled times there was scarce chance of schools operating normally, so Dominic received little formal education. His family was, like everyone else, adversely affected by the sacking of Youghal and it is likely that the disruption changed the course of Dominic's life. To stay in Ireland meant either converting to Protestantism or living the fragile life of a recusant. Dominic, even as a young man, was determinedly Catholic. He had dreamed of becoming a soldier, but he would have to join the Queen's forces supporting the Crown, or become a rebel, fighting outside the law for political and religious freedom. For different reasons, neither option attracted him. Instead he sailed for France, a tough, ambitious, hotheaded twenty-year-old, hungry for adventure. He found many opportunities for his military ambitions and spent much of the next decade honing his soldier's skills with more than a little success. Yet when he made the return journey to Youghal, it was not in the uniform of a soldier but in the habit of a Jesuit brother. He came home not as an avenging soldier but as a man transformed by the crucible of the battle-field into a gentle, prayerful, radiant missionary. His homecoming was to be bloody nonetheless.

Dominic arrived in France almost penniless. This meant that his ambition to be a soldier would have to be postponed until he had earned enough money to buy the arms, clothes and horse, which were essential if he was to become an officer. He took a job as a servant in a hostelry in Nantes, a town in Brittany in Northern France, and spent the next three years working in several inns, learning French and conscientiously saving his wages.

It was a time of single-minded dedication and eventually he had sufficient command of the French language and enough money to realise his dream. There was no shortage of armies to join, for France was convulsed by a civil war and the protagonists were divided along lines well known to Dominic. On one side were the Catholics and on the other the Protestants, though as in Ireland people were apt to change sides unexpectedly. Dominic became an officer in the army of Philip Emmanuel de Vaudemont, Duke de

Mercoeur, who was a member of the Holy League, an organisation set up to defend the Catholic Faith in France. The League was locked in battle with the Protestant Huguenots led by Henry of Navarre (later Henry IV, King of France), then a staunch Calvinist. Henry's claim to the throne of France was bitterly disputed by the League who supported their own Catholic candidate. Henry's religious disposition had all the certainty of a chameleon crawling across a rainbow. He was reared in the faith of his devoutly Protestant mother, briefly converted to Catholicism under duress and then changed back to Protestantism again. By 1593 he was once more a Catholic, although his reasons had more to do with making himself broadly acceptable to the people of France than with any real spiritual commitment.

Ireland was not the only country where the politico/religious landscape was in a tortuous knot. While Catholicism was being outlawed in Ireland and England, Protestantism was outlawed in France. Europe was in turmoil over religion and the fight was to drag on in Ireland into the twentieth century. In France however Henry IV, now a Catholic monarch, quickly defused the sectarian conflict which was draining his country by granting extensive civil and religious liberties to the Protestant Huguenots in 1598 through the Edict of Nantes.

As a young Irish officer, Dominic Collins spent nine years in the service of the Holy League. He did well, advancing to the rank of captain and becoming military governor of Lapena, a territory he took by force from Huguenot control. Henry of Navarre offered him 2,000 ducats, a small fortune, for the return of the castle at Lapena, but Dominic refused to have anything to do with Henry who was still a Protestant.

Gradually the power of the League began to diminish. It had been fuelled by opposition to a Protestant monarch but Henry's conversion to Catholicism in 1593 won over many former opponents, though Dominic, it seems, was not among them. Henry's dalliance with Rome was no comfort to the young captain. He believed that his faith was still very vulnerable, and his next career move seems to indicate that his military career was always more concerned with the protection of Catholicism than the amusement or advancement of Dominic Collins. The Spanish were active supporters of the League and they remained opposed to Henry. Dominic handed over the castle at Lapena to Don Juan del Aguila, a Spanish General. With letters of recommendation to the Spanish king from Aguila himself, he headed for Spain.

His ship put into shore near the northern port of San Sebastian and a new career in the Spanish military seemed to be certain. Dominic's letter of recommendation from Aguila and the intervention of Bishop Thady Farrell of Clonfert resulted in the offer of a pension of twenty-five crowns a month from the Spanish king. Away from the theatre of war, with time on his hands and now in a relatively safe environment, Dominic began to reflect deeply on his life and his future. Soldiering no longer held him in thrall. He had seen too much bloodshed and lived through too much political upheaval to be convinced that violence was the answer to the problems that concerned him. He realised he was at a turning point in his life.

For ten months he faced each day with dread and a heart full of doubt. It should have been the most restful time of his life, for there was no war to be fought, no battle to prepare for, and no money worries. Yet the quiet, insistent voice of God seemed to nag at him morning and night, urging him to take a critical look at the world around him and seek the way of prayer instead of the way of vengeance and might. Many times he went to confession to unburden the struggles going on in his soul. A number of confessors recognised the flowering of a vocation and were quick to offer him a place in their communities. He wasn't interested, but neither was he interested in doing more of what he had been doing. It wasn't just the privations of soldiering, or the dangers, but the coarseness of the life, the blunting of sensitivities that disgusted him more and more. Even the army chaplains struck him as ignorant lumps with little in their conduct to set them apart from the worst of the evil-tongued foot soldiers.

Fate brought him to Corunna, a naval base in northern Spain where many Irish soldiers were stationed. It was an ideal place to pick up news from home, for it was a popular landing place for travellers from Ireland.

It was the season of Lent in the spring of 1598. The Irish fleet had arrived at Corunna and Father White was in town to hear their confessions. He was an interesting man, passionately devoted to the welfare of the Irish in Spain. He had founded the Irish college in Salamanca when it became impossible for Catholics to get an education in Ireland. He and Dominic struck up a warm and immediate friendship. The disenchanted soldier related his scruples to Father White but this time it wasn't the confessor who pointed towards the priestly vocation but rather Dominic himself, and now it was the priest who shook his head in doubt. As soon as Dominic heard that father White was a Jesuit, he felt the jagged fragments inside himself suddenly slip comfortably into place. Now he knew with certainty that he had to be a Jesuit. He was overcome with an enthusiasm not shared by Father White. The Jesuits were formidably intellectual and highly educated. Dominic's lack of early education ruled out the Jesuit priesthood. It didn't matter, said Dominic, he would settle for the Jesuit brotherhood. Father White was sceptical. The Jesuit brothers did menial work not exactly suited to a man who was used to commanding troops and wearing an officer's uniform. Dominic's enthusiasm, however, was overwhelming. He wore down Father White's resistance until the latter agreed to write to the Jesuit Provincial on his behalf. The Provincial took one look at Dominic's career and his fiery personality and advised against such a curious change. Nevertheless, Dominic refused to go away. Letter after letter arrived from Corunna begging the Provincial to give him a chance. Finally he won his point. He was admitted to the Jesuit college in the great shrine city of Santiago de Compostela.

He packed his bags to leave Corunna where the story of his vocation had become the local soap opera. His soldier friends were stunned. Dominic had seemed to be the archetypal successful career soldier. He was at the top of his profession, he had a comfortable pension, people jumped to attention at his commands - and here he was going off to wash floors for the love of God. They were incredulous. So were the Jesuits when Dominic arrived wearing his captain's uniform on 8 December 1598.

It was the custom in the Jesuit college to record details of all new entrants and the archives show that a tall, handsome, thirty-two-year-old Irishman, the son of distinguished parents, was admitted into the Society of Jesus.

The quiet, prayerful life Dominic was looking for was slow to materialise. He had scarcely arrived when the novitiate was hit by an outbreak of fever that affected three brothers and four priests. Some of the more fearful novices fled in order to escape the disease. Dominic stood his ground and for two months he was doctor, nurse, cook and maid to his new Jesuit brethren.

Two years passed at the college during which Dominic settled into his humble role, though apparently not always with humility. His superiors were impressed by his strength and judgement but noted that he was "colerico y porfiado," in other words "bad-tempered and stubborn as a mule." Sooner or later chopping vegetables and slopping out cells was bound to get under the skin of someone as action oriented as Dominic. Still, he survived the ups and downs, learning to take them in his stride, and on the 4th of February he proudly made his first religious profession.

Suddenly Dominic's life was upended yet again when his Spanish superiors notified him in the summer after his profession that he had been appointed to a post back home in Ireland, companion to Father James Archer, the Jesuit chaplain to the Spanish forces, a man high on the English wanted list.

Once again, Ireland was in the throes of battle as the Ulster chieftains O'Neill and O'Donnell tried to rally a countrywide final push against the English. Father Archer was very knowledgeable about the political state of Ireland. He had taken messages from O'Neill to Rome and to Spain where he had begged the king for help. The new Spanish king, Philip III, finally agreed to send help to the native Irish. As Father Archer made his preparations, he gave some thought to a suitable companion. He didn't know Dominic, but from his contacts with the Jesuits and with Bishop Thady Farrell of Clonfert, he had more than likely heard quite a bit of tantalising gossip about the reformed soldier. Archer's work in Ireland was going to be dangerous. He needed someone who was physically and mentally fit, someone who knew Ireland and who would not become a burden when the going got tough. Dominic had no peer on all fronts. His name commended itself, despite his relative newness to the religious life.

Dominic sailed with the Spanish expedition from the Portuguese port of Belem, near Lisbon, on the 3rd September 1601. One of the expedition's two commanders was none other than Don Juan del Aguila, the man who had first encountered Dominic as a captain in the forces of the Holy League in northern France. Father Archer travelled in the flagship while Dominic sailed in one of the smaller vessels. They didn't have time to meet before the fleet set sail and it was five months later in a remote castle in Ireland that they first encountered each other face to face. By that time the course of Irish history had been decisively changed, though scarcely for the better.

It seems that each time the Spaniards set sail for Ireland, the elements conspired to raise every conceivable obstacle to their progress. The inevitable bad weather set in, scattering the fleet and separating Dominic's squadron from the main force. The bigger part of the expedition managed to get to Kinsale by 21 September. With little difficulty Kinsale fell into the hands of del Aguila and his three thousand soldiers. They settled in to wait for the arrival of O'Neill and O'Donnell who were marching from the north. Many other Irish chieftains were also en route to Kinsale for what they hoped would be the final and successful showdown against the Crown. Instead, it turned out to be a disaster of epic proportions, often characterised as the great missed opportunity and much lamented afterwards in song and story.

The English surrounded Kinsale, cutting the Spaniards off from the approaching Irish chieftains but also effectively sandwiching the Crown troops between two hostile armies. If anyone was at a disadvantage it should have been the English for they had, on the face of it, been checkmated. Historians have disputed the "whys" and the "if onlys" of the Battle of Kinsale, but whatever the reasons, the Irish lost, and lost badly. The Irish attack on the English troops was not supported from within Kinsale by the besieged Spaniards. Instead of being harried from the front and the rear, the Crown forces were attacked only from the front and by an army quite unused to taking the offensive. The attack, launched on Christmas Eve, was impressively countered by the English and the Irish chieftains were routed. They fled in disarray, some homewards, some to Spain to seek more help, some to regroup in the hope of fighting another day. Dominic Collins witnessed the Battle of Kinsale and no doubt, as a former successful soldier he despaired of the weaknesses in the Irish tactics and the indecision of the Spaniards.

Dominic had come to Kinsale in the company of the Irish chieftain, O'Sullivan Beare, who led an army drawn from

Kerry and West Cork. After the miserable battle, he stayed with O'Sullivan who was now desperate to get back to his home territory, the desolately beautiful Beara peninsula, and to defend it from the victorious English.

In the month of February, Father Archer and Dominic found themselves together for the first time at Gortnacloghy Castle, near Castlehaven, thirty miles to the West of Kinsale. The great plan to rouse all Ireland from its slumber was in tatters, and without considerable outside assistance the future looked decidedly grim. Del Aguila had made a very civilised deal with the Earl of Mountjoy, head of the English troops, under which the Spaniards were allowed to sail safely and happily for home. They did just that, though the homecoming was a frosty affair. The Spanish monarch was so outraged by del Aguila's conduct he had him arrested. Mercifully, the disgraced former commander did not have to suffer his fall from favour for long, for he died soon after his return.

There was no deal for the Irish chieftains. O'Sullivan was now being pursued by the Crown troops led by Sir George Carew and he made his stand at Dunboy Castle, strategically sited to protect the O'Sullivan territory. Situated on a magnificent but isolated promontory, the castle provided safety and shelter for Dominic and Father Archer, though both knew it was only a matter of time before the English arrived.

The Crown forces laid siege to Dunboy but it was a bitter, long drawn-out affair. The troops endured abysmal weather for months on end. The English commander, Sir George Carew, had curious ideas about the powers of the Jesuits. In a letter to Sir Robert Cecil he shows a tendency to hysterical superstition by blaming Archer for the diabolical weather:

"Archer the priest conjures the foul weather, which I do partly believe, for the old men have never seen the like in May. If he remains in Dunboy I hope to conjure his head in a halter. He hath a fellow devil to help him, one Dominic Collins, a friar, who in his youth was a scholar and brother to him that was this last year mayor of Youghal."

At first O'Sullivan Beare wasn't unduly worried about his situation. If he could keep the English engaged in the siege of Dunboy, it would give the other chieftains time to get themselves reorganised and to link up with fresh Spanish troops whose arrival was awaited imminently.

Dominic and Father Archer ministered spiritually to the beleaguered men, but as the weeks grew into months it became clear that there would be no more Spanish help. They were on their own, and time was running out. The English got ready for an all-out assault on the castle as soon as the weather cleared at the end of May. Carew's troops had already gained control of some of the little islands around Dunboy. They massacred three hundred women, children and old men on Dursey island alone, where O'Sullivan's small defensive force was overwhelmed. When the troops appeared on the beach outside Dunboy Castle, a fierce struggle broke out. Some of the Irish were driven back inside, Dominic among them. Others, including Father Archer, escaped to join O'Sullivan Beare who had already moved his camp some twenty miles away. Archer decided that he would try to reach Spain and rally the King to action once more. He escaped in a small open boat just as the English troops launched their final offensive against the castle. There was little hope for the one hundred and forty-three defenders of Dunboy.

Carew used heavy artillery to batter the castle's walls. It had taken the English several days to set up the guns, and during that time O'Sullivan Beare stood by with an army one thousand strong, but did nothing. Perhaps he still expected that the Spaniards would show up, but his delay cost him dearly. The castle was bombarded relentlessly by Carew's big guns. Part of it caved in on top of the occupants while the rest fought hand-to-hand defending their territory centimetre by centimetre in a battle of screaming savagery. Inside Dunboy the dead were piled high, and the wounded outnumbered the able-bodied. At last the survivors were all trapped in a basement from which escape was impossible. The English outside prepared for the final act.

Dominic was one of the few uninjured. He struggled out of the ruined building towards the English line bringing an offer of surrender provided that the lives of the occupants were guaranteed. Carew dismissed it out of hand, arrested him and commenced the final onslaught. He took seventy-three prisoners. Fifty-eight were marched immediately to the market square and summarily hanged. Twelve more met the same fate four days later. Three, including Dominic, were taken to Cork. The other two were executed there, but Dominic, after four months in Cork prison, was transported to Youghal so that his death would have the maximum impact.

Dominic had played no part in the fighting and his captors found him very open and forthcoming about his background and his reasons for being in Ireland. Carew interrogated him at great length. His so-called "detestable treasons" consisted of accompanying the Spaniards to Ireland and being in the garrison at Dunboy, but Carew's real motive for holding on to Dominic longer than any other prisoner was very simple. He hoped to exert enough pressure to get him to renounce his faith and his membership in the Jesuit Order. An ex-Jesuit turned loyalist would be a very desirable commodity and particularly useful in the propaganda war against the Roman Catholic Church.

During his four months in jail, Dominic was subjected to a well-orchestrated and relentless campaign to make him renounce his faith. A tribe of visitors offered him inducements, bribes and threats. His family, terrorised by the prospect of his execution, pleaded with him to cooperate with Carew. There was physical abuse too, but nothing had any effect on him. Dominic was a former soldier, after all, well used to facing death in one violent form or another. Now he had chosen the path of Christ and he felt privileged to be dying for a cause in which he so strongly believed. Carew's hopes for Dominic's conversion to Protestantism did not materialise. In his dealings with the Jesuit brother, Carew was impressed by him, but not sufficiently impressed to give him back his life. A court martial ordered his execution.

On Sunday 31st October Dominic awoke to face his day of martyrdom. He was in high spirits. He dressed in his Jesuit cassock and walked to the scaffold joyfully. Kneeling before the gallows he exclaimed, "Hail, Holy Cross so long desired by me." When an English officer remarked on his good humour, Dominic stunned him and his audience with his reply: "For this cause I would be willing to die not once but a thousand deaths." The impact of his serene demeanour was felt most keenly by the hangman who could not bring himself to do his job. The crowd grew jittery, but Dominic calmed them with his prayerfulness. He told them of his faith in the Church founded by Christ and of his delight in dying for it. A fisherman who happened to be in the crowd was seized by the soldiers and told to carry out the execution. The poor man was almost demented with fear. He begged Dominic to forgive him. Brother Dominic did so warmly, placed the noose around his own neck and mounted the ladder reciting a psalm. He had just spoken the words "Into your hands, O Lord, I commend my spirit" when the temporary executioner pulled away the ladder. Dominic's body dropped down into the void. He was left to dangle there for three of four hours. The unfortunate fisherman was unable to finish the job of quartering the body, and there was no one willing to undertake the task. Suddenly the rope snapped and Dominic's body fell to the ground, landing in a kneeling position as if he was simply deep in prayer.

Carew's menacing spectacle had been something of a propaganda failure, but to retrieve the situation, at least a little, he ordered Dominic's body to be stripped and left naked to be jeered at by the crowd. When night came, the inevitable group of good Catholics saw to it that his body was interred close to the place of execution, after a dignified religious ceremony.

The body of Dominic Collins was barely cold when the story of his death travelled along the Jesuit circuit throughout Europe. Stories of miracles he had worked appeared soon after, and an oil portrait of him, painted in the 1620s, found its way back to Ireland. It still hangs today in St. Patrick's College, Maynooth.

CHAPTER 7

Bishop Conor O'Devany and Father Patrick O'Loughran

Martyred together in Dublin, 1st February 1612

On the north side of Dublin's river Liffey, not far from the City Centre, there is a small residential enclave known as O'Devany Gardens. Until the promotion of the martyrs' cause began in earnest in the late 1980s, it is unlikely that many, if any, of the residents of the street had much idea of the reasons why their street bore the name O'Devany. The man in question had been dead for almost four centuries and during his lifetime had been bishop of the northern diocese of Down and Connor, one hundred miles away. I who was born and reared in the heart of that diocese had never heard his name mentioned, even though the names of those who tormented and eventually killed him were and are celebrated in the street names of Belfast, the city at the core of Down and Connor. Yet somewhere in the vague mists of Dublin's folklore, the story of this tragic elderly prelate had been carefully preserved and handed on from generation to generation, ending up as a label on a gable wall, almost but not quite forgotten. There is a sense of justice about his vindication as a martyr even after all these lost years, for it is probable, according to the contemporary historian John McCavitt, that O'Devany was the most historically significant of the martyrs, perhaps of even greater significance than Saint Oliver Plunket. It is also poignantly ironic that Conor O'Devany was the author of the Index Martyrialis, a list of all the priests and lay people who had died for their faith, and itself an important source of information about many of his fellow martyrs.

Conor O'Devany was an Ulsterman, born in the parish of Glenfin, County Donegal, the most westerly and most ruggedly beautiful of the northern counties. He grew up in a family whose links to the Church were not just strong but special, for he was a member of an "aircheannach" (as it is written in Gaelic) or erenagh family. Each parish had its erenagh, a layman who played a central role in the structure and management of parish affairs. He traditionally rented and farmed Church lands and assumed responsibility for the maintenance of Church property. Often the erenagh was an erudite and educated man who actively assisted in the education of young priests. It was hardly surprising then that many vocations to the priesthood came from within the erenagh family, for family life revolved around and was enmeshed in the daily life of the Church. Conor O'Devany was one such vocation.

Though we know relatively little about his childhood in the diocese of Raphoe, County Donegal, the infant Conor arrived into a world seething with religious and political upheaval. The precise date of his birth is not known, but it was close to that cathartic day in 1534 when Henry VIII, infuriated by Pope Clement VII's refusal to grant him an annulment, scorned allegiance to Rome and set himself up as Supreme Head of the newly-created Anglican Church. With bishops and priests from Donegal and Derry (many of them relations) as regular visitors to his home, the stormy politics of the times were much discussed at the O'Devany table. Even so, Reformation and Counter-Reformation seemed reasonably distant concerns in that remote corner of Ireland. Its very geography nourished conservatism, and deep-rooted tradition flourished there still.

About the year 1550, in his late teens, Conor joined the Franciscan order at the Observant friary in Donegal. It was an interesting choice and says something about the commitment of the young Conor to authentic Christian values and genuine spirituality. The fifteenth century was characterised by a determination among the Irish monastic community to reform and shake itself out of the decay and lethargy into which it had fallen. The "Observant" reform movement was the vehicle of change. It received overwhelming popular support, with many old monastic houses adopting it, new ones springing up all over the country, and a reinvigoration of lay participation particularly in the Third Order of St. Francis. The Franciscan house in Donegal was established in 1474 by the ruling O'Donnell family during that period of unrivalled regeneration.

There were bad days ahead in which the monasteries would be attacked and demolished in the war against Catholicism, but those days had not yet arrived when Conor submitted himself to the rigorous life of an Observant Franciscan. The friary was then full to capacity, a hive of spiritual activity.

As Conor settled down to the day-to-day life of a friar he can have had little idea of the role he was to play in bringing the Counter-Reformation into the mainstream of Irish life, nor of the appalling sacrifice he would make in doing so. Yet in many ways the signs were already there. The conflict between the state religion and the Church of Rome was worsening. The government was determined to stamp its authority on all aspects of worship. The monasteries were in the front line and the Observant friars became resolute defenders of the traditional Faith. In Donegal as elsewhere there must have been endless hours of debate on the state efforts to abolish the Mass and impose a common form of worship, as well as constant fears for the safety of the monastery in the growing climate of hostility to "papishness". The young friar was doubtless reassured by the Catholic Queen Mary's assumption of the throne in 1553, but the security was short-lived. Conor entered his twenties just as Ireland began a scandalous century of blood-letting. The battle for English, Protestant political and religious control of the Irish Catholic people was about to be well and truly declared.

Elizabeth I became Queen in 1558 on the death of her half-sister, Mary. They had hardly exemplified sisterly devotion. Elizabeth was the daughter of Anne Boleyn, Henry VIII's controversial second wife. Mary was the daughter of his first marriage to the Spanish princess, Catherine of Aragon, whom he had summarily divorced after the Pope refused to annul the marriage. Mary's life was a tale of tragic reversals. Her father's attempts to annul the marriage to her mother placed her under the cloud of illegitimacy. She was kept away from her mother and treated appallingly by Anne Boleyn, though Henry eventually became reconciled to his eldest daughter and restored her right to succeed to the throne.

During Mary's reign Elizabeth had been imprisoned in the Tower of London and Mary's emphatic, often violent reinstatement of Roman Catholicism (she has gone down in history as "Bloody Mary") had been hard on Elizabeth's supporters. Now that Elizabeth was monarch (and certainly no less bloody than her half-sister), the pendulum predictably swung forcefully back to Protestantism. In 1560, the English Parliament enacted the Act of Succession and the Act of Uniformity under which it was no longer possible to remain faithful to Rome while at the same time acknowledging the sovereignty of the Queen. Fidelity to Rome at any level was treachery, according to the law, and the government was bent on eradicating it. Rome, for its part, was no passive observer. The outside world was closing in like a vice on the remote Donegal monastery where Conor lived the simple, hard life of a devout friar. The Pope and the Queen of England were at loggerheads as the Queen's agents tightened their control on Irish worship and began their systematic attempts to abolish Catholicism. In response, Pope

Gregory XIII appointed a team of Irish bishops to provide pastoral backbone to the beleaguered Catholic people. Conor O'Devany was one of these new bishops. His consecration as Bishop of the diocese of Down and Connor took place in the German national church of Santa Maria dell'Anima in Rome on the 13th May 1582. The ceremony was conducted by the Cardinal Protector of Ireland, Nicholas de Pelleve, Archbishop of Sens. The archives recording Conor's appointment indicate that the circumstances of his birth had created an impediment to his consecration, which required a formal dispensation "super defectu nataliam". Just what the defect was is not known, but it is likely that his parents' marriage was regarded as void under Canon Law because of the degree of consanguinity. Such marriages, between closely related cousins, were very commonplace, particularly in the quasi-tribal clan-based system of Gaelic Ireland. It is also possible that his father was a priest (again a not uncommon occurrence), in which case the dispensation would have been necessary. Conor was the third Franciscan in a row to be appointed bishop of Down and Connor, and he returned to the diocese immediately after his consecration.

The new bishop's work was clear. The tide of state Protestantism was to be resisted in Ulster by the dedicated teaching of the doctrines of the Council of Trent. The Council had not only reformed and updated the Church, but had painstakingly countered each of the points of doctrinal conflict raised by Protestantism. There were others who planned to respond to the violence of the government with retaliation in kind, but Conor O'Devany was not among them. In 1587, he and six fellow bishops attended a synod in the diocese of Clogher (also in Ulster) where they laid plans for the promulgation of the decrees of the Council of Trent throughout the northern dioceses. The news of their meeting and their plans provoked more than a little worry and annoyance among the state authorities, who were unable or unwilling to distinguish between political and religious activity. Since in their own case the two were fused like inseparable Siamese twins, they saw this development as evidence of further rebellious foment in Ulster.

At every turn Bishop O'Devany was in danger of arrest. The authorities did not simply dislike Roman Catholic clerics. Their intemperate language in letters of the period shows a searing sectarian hatred. The Catholic primate of Ireland, Archbishop Creagh of Armagh, had been arrested in the 1570s and held in prison for many years. Rome appointed Redmond O'Gallagher, Bishop of Derry, to act temporarily in place of the primate, but he too was constantly under threat. In July 1588, with the entire country in a state of high nervous tension because of the failure of the Spanish Armada, and anticipating that he too would soon be arrested, O'Gallagher wrote to Conor O'Devany, delegating to him the primate's powers of absolution and dispensation. As it happened, the Bishop of Down and Connor was no more immune from arrest than the Bishop of Derry. The letter was in Conor O'Devany's pocket when he himself was arrested a short time later during the blanket sweep of the country which followed the defeat of the Armada. The aim was to cleanse Ireland of committed Catholics.

Chained up in the freezing cold of Dublin Castle, Bishop O'Devany endured four intensely miserable years. Under the prison rules no food, clothing or water was supplied to prisoners except that brought to them by their families and friends. Conor was over a hundred miles away from his home and he had neither contacts nor money. He came very close to dying from hunger and thirst, but thanks to his own resourcefulness and the common humanity of his fellow prisoners he survived, though greatly enfeebled by the harshness of the prison conditions.

In November 1590 O'Devany submitted a petition for his release. It was a masterfully constructed document, probably written with experienced help and advice from Catholic lawyers, for it cleverly exploited both the political and legal weaknesses of the day. He promised to "behave himself as becomes the dutiful subject. . ." but nowhere in the document did he take the oath of supremacy acknowledging the Queen as head of the Church. The petition came before the three commissioners for ecclesiastical causes: Lancaster, the Protestant Archbishop of Armagh, Jones, the Protestant Bishop of Meath, and Loftus, the Lord Chancellor and Protestant Archbishop of Dublin. All three men were capable of the vilest acts, but there was a large measure of uncertainty about the effects of persecuting Catholic clergy too ardently. Conor O'Devany benefited from their ambivalence on this occasion and was released in 1592. Almost immediately Loftus found himself accused of going soft on Catholics because he had unlawfully released "a Romish bishop." In his own defence, Loftus decided to gild the lily by falsely claiming that O'Devany had not only taken the oath of supremacy but was willing to spy on behalf of the government. "O'Devany", wrote Loftus, "willinnglie submitted himself not onely to take the oathe of supremacye, but also tooke his corporall oathe ever afterwards to become his majesty's true and faithfull subject and espetially in this - that he sholde riveall unto the Lord Deputy and Councell from tyme to tyme anie forrayn or Domesticall practice against his majesty. or this estate, coming to his knowledge, which oathe he tooke with a moste earnest protestation of his good and true meaning to serve his majesty for which respect I and the rest were moved to take compassion of his miserable estate ..."

Curiously, or perhaps not so curiously, Loftus was unable to produce any document in which Bishop O'Devany took the oath of supremacy.

Conor made his way northwards back to his diocese where hearts were hardening rapidly against the English. The northern clans were being pushed to their limits. When the most hesitant of them, the O'Neill of Tyrone, decided that he would be pushed no further and would take to arms, he fused a powerful alliance with the other chieftains. At its zenith, it looked as if the alliance could turn the tide of history in favour of the native Irish and their preferred religion. Towards the end of 1592, when war seemed likely, the bishops met in the west of Ulster to review the deteriorating situation. They decided to ask Philip II of Spain for help. The driving force behind the bishops' meeting was the new primate, Archbishop Edmund Magauran of Armagh. Conor O'Devany had been away from the scene for a long time and could not have emerged from prison in the best of health, so it is likely that he was not at the meeting. Later he was to deny vehemently any suggestion that he took part in the ensuing war. His denial was all the more credible because of the somewhat scathing criticism of him made by Peter Lombard, the former O'Neill agent who became Archbishop of Armagh during the heady days of 1601. Conor "was a good man but an innocent," said Peter, "from whom no great help can be expected." He was probably right on all counts, for when O'Neill went to O'Devany asking for help in his crusade against the English domination, the bishop refused point-blank to have anything to do with military or political affairs.

In early 1603, the Ulster chieftains gave up their military crusade and admitted defeat. They had one piece of luck, however, in what was otherwise a fiasco, for Queen Elizabeth died only days before O'Neill's formal surrender. Instead of the punitive terms the Irish chieftains might have expected, their lands were not confiscated. The new monarch, James I, was the son of one of the most controversial and intriguing characters of the period, Mary Queen of Scots, who had been imprisoned and finally beheaded by Elizabeth because as a Catholic she was seen to pose a threat to English Protestantism. The Irish hoped that James might be inclined to ease off on the harsh imposition of English Protestantism, for he himself was deeply attracted to doctrinal

Presbyterianism rather than Anglicanism. He had become King of Scotland at the tender age of one after his mother was deposed. He never set eyes on her again and seems to have harboured very little affection for her if one is to judge by his failure to intervene convincingly with Elizabeth when Mary was sentenced to death. From an early age his eyes were firmly set on the throne of England, for Elizabeth was childless and James was her nearest heir. He came to the throne with an inflated sense of his own destiny and greatness and with no love of Catholicism. Any hopes of a benign reign were annihilated when a Royal proclamation in 1605 ordered all Jesuits and seminary priests to leave the kingdom and required all laity to attend Protestant worship. The consequences for failure to comply were drastic.

Conor O'Devany was now an elderly man in his seventies, running out of energy and safe hiding places. By his very presence in Ireland he was breaking the king's law, and to survive at all he often had to resort to disguises. The Ulster chieftains were able to provide him with only limited protection, for they too were under constant pressure and harassment by the military and state authorities. Conor managed to avoid capture for a time with the help of the O'Donnells, but the authorities were on his heels. Indeed, George Montgomery, the Protestant bishop of the northern dioceses of Derry, Raphoe and Clogher, was actively engaged in trying to establish O'Devany's whereabouts and was raising alarm in the Pale about what might happen if he was left to roam about the country. There was speculation that he might be headed for Spain to plead the cause of the chieftains, but his age makes the claim seem as futile as it is unlikely.

The 4th September 1607, marks the date of one of Ireland's saddest hours, when the great Ulster chieftains, among them the legendary Hugh O'Neill, left Ireland for ever, so great was their despair of ever achieving freedom in their own country. If Conor had been concerned for his own safety, he could presumably have accompanied the earls into exile. He chose not to go. Soon after, he was appointed vice-primate of Ireland, but the new office only increased his chances of being arrested. His protectors were all gone and the primate himself, Peter Lombard, was in Rome. Conor was in the front line and defenceless.

In 1610, he made a pilgrimage to Monahincha, near Roscrea, County Tipperary. It had been designated a place of pilgrimage by Pope Paul V a few years earlier and had drawn thousands of faithful Catholics to it in the intervening period. Conor, making no concession to his advancing years, made the pilgrimage barefoot. He was not just on a private visit, however. In parishes the length and breadth of the country the open, normal practice of the faith was becoming more difficult and dangerous with each passing day. Pilgrimages, on the other hand, provided an ideal opportunity to administer the sacraments to large numbers of people. They also frightened the devil out of the Protestant establishment. On his visit to Monahincha, the sacrament of Confirmation would have been high on Conor's list of priorities, and while other priests performed weddings, baptisms and heard confessions, it is certain that the Bishop of Down and Connor, by now one of only two Catholic bishops remaining in Ireland, spent much of his time conferring the gifts of the Holy Spirit, of grace, strength and courage, on both adults and children. Given the times the people of Ireland were living in, this was certainly an appropriate sacrament to administer.

The making of the pilgrimage to Monahincha was no easy thing to do. The road was long, and fraught with dangers. Many of the women pilgrims were brutally assaulted by marauding soldiers from nearby garrisons. For a man nearing eighty, it was a measure of Conor's own enduring courage and fortitude that he was able to make it at all.

His life now was devoted, in between furtive pastoral activity, to compiling his Index Martyrialis, a vital contemporary record of the people who were dying and had died for their faith in his time. In a final twist of fate, it was to be an important document in processing the causes of a number of his fellow martyrs. He completed his work in the early part of 1611 and sent a copy to the Jesuits. Just in time, for in that summer the king's men caught up with him at the home of Brian MacHugh óg MacMahon, the son-in-law of Hugh O'Neill. Bishop O'Devany was visiting MacMahon's home on a specific pastoral mission rather than simply in search of refuge, though, in truth, there were few places left where he could safely find shelter. A family squabble had arisen within MacMahon's clan and the bishop came to act as mediator in the hope of settling it. Inter-family quarrels were commonplace, but in the light of what was happening throughout the country the bishop very likely found such family feuds an unseemly and unchristian waste of energy and resources. The soldiers who arrested him came upon him quite by chance, but there was much jubilation in Dublin at his capture. He was the most senior cleric to fall into Crown hands for quite some time. They took him to Dublin and imprisoned him in Dublin Castle once more. The closing chapter of his life was now to be linked with that of a young priest whom he had never met before, Father Patrick O'Loughran, who was, like many of his clerical contemporaries, languishing in jail waiting to see what the authorities had in mind for him.

Patrick O'Loughran was an Ulsterman, from County Armagh, and like Conor O'Devany he came from an erenagh family which had provided many priests to the diocese of Armagh. His actual name was a variant of Patrick Giolla Phádraig, which means the servant of Patrick. Judging by the date of his birth, in or around 1577, he was ordained during the war year. O'Loughran had been chaplain to both Hugh O'Neill and his wife, the Countess of Tyrone. It was a job which went with being the son of an erenagh in the territory of the O'Neill, for Patrick's family home at Donaghmore was in the O'Neill mensal lands. There would have been little choice in the matter, and when O'Neill decided rather suddenly to join the other earls in their flight to the European mainland in 1607, his former chaplain, now jobless, sailed to Flanders hoping to further his studies there. He became a student at the Irish College at Douai and made a visit to Rome, possibly hoping to meet up with O'Neill, sometime in 1608. He was delighted, while there, to have the opportunity to kneel before the Pope.

In 1611, Patrick O'Loughran decided to return to Ireland. He had been awarded a benefice in County Louth and perhaps wished to take it up, though his full reasons for leaving the relative safety of Douai are not clearly known. Alerted by his spies, Lord Deputy Chichester, the President of Munster, was waiting for him as soon as he disembarked in Cork in the month of June. Chichester's favourite occupation for some time had been the pursuing and hanging of Catholic priests. Under questioning by the Lord President, Patrick openly admitted that he was a priest and former chaplain to the O'Neills. He was taken directly either to Dublin Castle or to the common criminal prison, where he joined many other clerics in captivity.

Not all the imprisoned clerics were regarded in the same light by Chichester. Some were of Old English background, and while Chichester had no fondness for them, the authorities were to some extent anxious to try to appease and win them over. But a continental-trained Gaelic priest from rebellious Ulster, and especially one who had ministered to the much loathed Hugh O'Neill, was just the type to bring out the worst in the Lord Deputy.

Today's Royal Courts of Justice in Belfast are situated at the end of Chichester Street, right in the heart of the Diocese of Down and Connor. A few years ago one could drive past them or around them, park beside them, and wander into them. Today they are protected behind reinforced screening. Access is severely restricted in order to protect the judges (a number of whom have been violently murdered) and court personnel as well as the buildings themselves, which have been blasted to bits several times over the past two and a half decades. One wonders if Arthur, Lord Chichester, after whom the street is named, is any wiser today than he was then. At the time, his obsession to acquire wealth and power led him to seize the lands and property of the Catholic gentry, including a place well known to the contemporary world as Belfast's famous Falls Road. Such actions, and those of other English soldiers of fortune let loose to plunder Ireland in the name of the English Crown, are known by their historical, heavily pasteurised word, "plantation."

The Lord Deputy's particular preoccupation with priests who had trained abroad was centred on their commitment to the Counter-Reformation. He liked to describe them with colourful turns of phrase. Such priests were "hellish," "viperous" and in his most agreeable mood, "caterpillars." Their training was, in his view, designed to do nothing more than "raise commotions here where the Pope has more hearts than the king." Chichester's aversion was not of course peculiar to him alone. It was a widespread and strongly held view among Protestants in England and Ireland. Chichester was champing at the bit to ratchet up the repression. He had no time for more reasoned arguments, which advised that vigorous action against the priests would be counterproductive. Chichester belonged to the stamp-it-out-the-harder-the-better brigade.

In April 1611, King James I ordered Chichester to make sure that there was a "uniform order set down for the suppression of papistry." This enigmatic order required a clarification, which Chichester duly sought. He got his answer in August when he was told that it might be useful and timely to impose exemplary punishment on some titular bishops, provided that the facts could be twisted to show political rather than religious transgression. There was a chronic shortage of available bishops. Apart from Conor

O'Devany and Archbishop Kearney of Cashel, there was not in all of Ireland another Catholic bishop to be found. Since Bishop O'Devany was already conveniently lodged in Dublin Castle, the field narrowed down to him. Although he was eighty years old, he was about to be charged with treason. Father O'Loughran commended himself because, like O'Devany, he had a connection to the Ulster chieftains. From this Chichester believed he could fashion a case of guilt-by-association.

Conditions in prison for the two men were appalling. Their hardship was somewhat relieved from time to time by visits from Dublin's Catholic citizenry and a few Franciscans who were, despite the dangers, able to bring them the necessary materials for saying Mass.

Chichester's strategy began with threats and cajoleries intended to persuade his prisoners to take the oath of supremacy. Both men were offered not just their lives but preferment as well if they would submit to the religious authority of the king. They refused, and their refusal gave Chichester the problem of deciding what to do next. He was under orders to make an example of a bishop, but he had to proceed in a way which had at least the vague facade of legitimacy about it. In December he made up his mind to proceed with charges of treason, since this was the only offence which would safely guarantee the death penalty.

The procedure for bringing a charge of treason was as heavy on formality as it was light on due process and concern for human rights. As a preliminary to the full hearing, a grand jury was summoned in the district where the crime was thought to have been committed. Its function was to see if there was evidence of the offence strong enough to justify a trial. The members of the jury were often handpicked by the government. They received virtually all their information from government sources and were generally directed to the verdict they were expected to find. The accused was not allowed any legal representation, though the Crown's case was of course argued by experienced lawyers.

It took a month to assemble a suitable jury. It met on a wintry morning in January in Newry, County Down, on the southern-most edge of Ulster. This was the place where O'Devany's treason allegedly arose. It was the nearest he was to get to his diocese of Down and Connor, a few miles farther north.

The grand jury obligingly found that there was evidence of treason in that O'Devany had aided and abetted Hugh O'Neill and "other most wicked traitoures." The finding was delivered hastily to Dublin and the prisoner was charged on 22 January 1612 in the court of king's bench. The full trial was set for 28th January. The senior presiding judge was one Dominic Sarsfield, a member of the Old English establishment, regarded by the native Irish as a most loathsome traitor himself and a man of utterly evil disposition. Throughout the trial he constantly hectored and abused the accused, though the court did accede to O'Devany's request that he be addressed by his religious title and not in the derogatory terms initially used by the judges. Both men pleaded not guilty, and the twelve-man jury was sworn in to try both men separately. There was only one Irishman among the twelve. The rest were either English or Scots, their sympathies already a foregone conclusion. The courtroom was packed to capacity and the atmosphere was dramatically tense. After all, this was to be a show trial, a major public relations exercise designed to strike sheer terror into the recusant population.

O'Devany had no lawyer and was not entitled to call any wit-nesses in his defence, yet he showed remarkable legal skill in han-dling his own case, so much so that given the help he received many years earlier from Dublin lawyers, it seems entirely proba-ble that he was very well prepared with similar help this time. He frankly admitted that he had lived in turbulent Ulster during the

THE 17 IRISH MARTYRS

war but pointed out that he did so because that was his diocese and his job as bishop was to minister to the pastoral needs of his people.

Contemporary accounts of the trials survived quite by chance when the papers were included in a book of precedents designed to help lawyers in the conduct of similar trials. They bear little resemblance to modern images of trials in which defendants are protected by a battery of due process rights, represented by trained advocates and judged by randomly selected jurors and credible judges. O'Devany and O'Loughran were subjected to a form of lawful kangaroo court, where the dice were loaded from the outset. The judges were committed in advance to obtaining a verdict of guilty, and the dialogue was just for show. Both priests denied any wrongdoing or any association with political or military activity. They left the court in no doubt that the only evidence against them was of the practice of their faith and their allegiance to Rome. True to his orders, Sarsfield was delighted to pass the death sentences. The date of execution was set for 1st February.

Visitors to Bishop O'Devany's cell were surprised to find him in great spirits and very relieved that he was not to end his days rotting in prison. He remarked that he had not felt as well in ten years, and his only wish was to be buried in his beloved Franciscan habit, which mattered more to him than his bishop's insignia.

The first of February came all too quickly. It was a typical, miserable, brooding Irish day. A blanket of cloud hung over the city as the prisoners were handed into the custody of the sheriff in the midafternoon. They arrived at the place of execution, lying face upwards in a cart, their bodies bound by ropes. Conor's Franciscan habit was worn under other clothing at the insistence of the authorities, but he bore this last indignity with equanimity, even managing to remark how fortunate he was to be transported to his death, while Christ had been forced to carry his own Cross. George's Hill, less than a mile from the Castle on the north side of the River Liffey, was the site on which they were to die. The scene was bizarre. Along the route were Protestant ministers calling on the condemned men to give up their faith in the Catholic Church and save themselves from the gallows. A more important sign of what was to follow was the huge number of Catholics who came to support the bishop and his young companion. They were in an angry mood, and they were there in their thousands. Many were so incensed that the death sentence had been passed on so old and obviously innocent a man that they were there to confess their faith in public for the first time after many years of dissembling. O'Devany's death was to be cathartic, and the signs were visible as he was pulled from the cart. An attempt was made to rescue him and might have succeeded, but the bishop himself pleaded with the crowd to let the execution continue. He raised his bound hands in blessing and asked them to remain constant in their love of the Catholic faith.

The Irish executioner accurately judged the temper of the crowd and disappeared, terrified of what would befall him if he had a hand in killing O'Devany. A substitute was hastily arranged. An Englishman serving time in jail for murder, was persuaded to do the job in exchange for a promise that he would not be executed himself. The sheriff nervously ordered the two prisoners to come forward to the gallows. Soldiers held the crowd back as Conor O'Devany removed the garment covering his Franciscan habit. He handed his Franciscan cowl to a woman friend who had visited him in prison and to whom he had entrusted his burial instructions.

Patrick O'Loughran, showing great fortitude, insisted that the bishop should go first so that he would have a priest to minister to him at his final moments. Conor, on the other hand, was afraid that the young priest would disintegrate emotionally when he saw the death that awaited him and so begged to go second so that he could encourage Patrick throughout the ordeal. Finally it was agreed that Conor should die first. As he slowly mounted the scaffold, Luke Chalenor, a Protestant minister, begged him to acknowledge his treason and ask for pardon. Conor replied that he had committed no treason and was being killed for his faith in the Catholic Church alone. The proof was that all he had to do was to acknowledge the king as head of the Church in order to go free. He had been made that offer a hundred times, and a hundred times he had turned it down. Chalenor offered to pray with him but Conor declined and prayed by himself. By the time he reached the top of the scaffold, his prayers had become a rallying cry to the assembled faithful. He exhorted them to persevere in their faith and to pray for those who persecuted them. He prayed that those who had abused him would return to the faith of their forefathers, and he forgave them for all they had done to him. The soldiers tried to stop him. Clearly what he had to say was not acceptable to the authorities. He offered his forgiveness to the nervous hangman, kissed the rope solemnly and placed it around his neck. Suddenly, the sun burst through the dark clouds and a red glow cascaded over the gallows as his body dropped down. As he hung lifeless from the rope, the sun disappeared again and the gloom descended. Now his aged body was disembowelled before the stunned assembly. The words "Behold the head of a traitor" rang out as his head was severed from his body. The executioner set the head to one side as he prepared to cut the corpse into quarters. Moments later the head was gone, rescued by a mourner and never to be recovered, despite a very sizeable reward for its return.

The crowd, by now almost demented, grabbed every available part of the bishop's clothes and body, proclaiming them the sanctified remains of a martyr. It was a far from edifying sight and cannot have done much to give courage to the waiting Patrick O'Loughran. The normally timorous young man found a strength he did not know he possessed. Firmly reciting the canticle, *Nunc dimittis*, he walked calmly to his death. Like Conor before him, he blessed the crowd before surrendering himself to the horrific fate that lay immediately before him. Once again the grief-stricken crowd surged forward to seize what they could of his earthly remains. The soldiers tried to stop it and in the melee quite a few people were injured.

All through the night the people kept a vigil, praying and singing. In the morning the Crown officials buried what remained of the bodies beside the scaffold, but the next night twelve young Catholic men stealthily dug up the remains and buried them with enormous reverence according to Catholic Church rites in a secret grave reserved for martyrs. To this day the location of the grave is unknown.

Conor O'Devany's martyrdom was instantly acknowledged and his relics were quickly brought to places all over Europe. A man whose arm was paralysed experienced an instant cure as he participated in the vigil that followed the bishop's death on George's Hill. It was the first of many miracles attributed to the elderly Franciscan.

More than thirty years later Dionisio Massart, who later became the secretary of the Sacred Congregation for the Propagation of the Faith, was spending a night as the guest of Robert Nugent at Carlanstown, County Westmeath. He was startled to be shown a severed head, which he wrote had "eyes, skin and hair, still fresh as if the head had been severed from the shoulders that very hour." The mysterious disappearance of Conor O'Devany's head had at last been solved.

Once again the authorities had been guilty of poor judgement. The death of the two priests was supposed to quell the most fervent Catholic heart and to intimidate the weak. It had just the opposite effect. So indignant and outraged were the Catholics of the Pale that their resolve strengthened. The Old English Catholics embraced the Counter-Reformation and despite the increasing harshness of the repression, they fought tooth and nail against every government attempt to obliterate Catholicism. Chichester was dumbfounded by the extent of the reaction he had unwittingly induced, and Parliament was so hesitant to impose more restrictive measures that all plans to increase the penal legislation were effectively scuttled.

Conor O'Devany's death was a catalyst within the Counter-Reformation movement in Ireland, though his vital contribution has been obscured by the prominence of the last Irish bishop martyred for his faith, Saint Oliver Plunkett. Now, however, Conor O'Devany is being rescued from oblivion by contemporary historians, anxious to place him in the centre of the Counter-Reformation stage where he truly belongs. The pastoral backbone Conor had come to Down and Connor to instil became his bequest to the people of the Pale. In his life he was a patient and self-effacing man, and in death he remained the same - waiting four hundred years for official recognition of his martyrdom, stepping aside to permit Oliver Plunkett to be the first Irish martyr canonised.

As for Arthur Chichester, the burghers of Belfast chose to ignore, or to conveniently forget that the man whose memory they cherish was ignominiously recalled to London in 1614 and pensioned off under a cloud of disgrace.

CHAPTER 8

Francis Taylor, Statesman

Died a martyr in prison in Dublin,
30th January 1621

The tidal wave of Catholic assertiveness which flowed from Conor O'Devany's death, gathered up many in its path. Francis Taylor was one of those energised and renewed in his faith at the outrage provoked by the bishop's death. The callousness of the executions concentrated the minds of the silent faithful. They could cower in terror as it was intended that they should, or they could challenge the government's tightening control on the practice and expression of Catholic beliefs. Francis Taylor had had enough. He became a voice of the voiceless, an outstanding leader of the recusant community in the Pale, chosen for his integrity and his uncompromising determination to use all lawful means to fight for Catholic religious freedom.

Francis Taylor's life is not unlike that of Margaret Ball, and though there are no records showing that their paths crossed, given their backgrounds and beliefs and the many ways in which their lives travelled the same road, it seems more likely than not that they were well acquainted. Like Margaret, Francis was born just outside Dublin, in the Pale's rural hinterland. His home town was Swords, north County Dublin, which today lies just north of the International airport. His parents, Robert Taylor and

Elizabeth Golding, had only two sons, Thomas, the firstborn, and Francis. They were wealthy landowners and the two boys were reared with the comfort and confidence one would expect of the affluent and influential.

Francis was born in 1550, by which time his father had already established a distinguished career as a bailiff of the City of Dublin. He was certainly one of the leading citizens of his day. The Taylor family were fervent Catholics. When Margaret Ball was imprisoned for her recusant activities, the Taylor family's vulnerability to prosecution was heightened too. No doubt her fate, and the role played by her estranged son Walter, were discussed many times and with great passion in the Taylor home.

Through those difficult years, however, the Taylor fortunes continued to prosper, though they never wavered in their allegiance to the Catholic Church, even when the nasty consequences of that allegiance became harsher and harsher. Like so many of their friends, they struggled to come to terms with the political allegiance they felt and continued to offer to the English authorities and the religious allegiance they gave to the Pope. As the pressures increased, however, they found themselves forced to fuse their political allegiance with faith in a newly-constructed state religion or suffer severe penalties. They then made their choice to resist the imposition of the Protestant faith, and to do so emphatically.

Thomas, the elder son, turned his back on the wealth and status which was his by birth and went to the continent to study for the priesthood. He became a convinced Counter-Reformationist and an acknowledged clerical scholar. His priestly vocation took him to England, where as a missionary in the 1580s he lived through some of the worst anti-Catholic excesses. He was finally arrested and sentenced to death for preaching against Elizabeth's state religion, but on the very threshold of martyrdom he was suddenly reprieved, to the immense relief of his family and in particular his younger brother.

Francis, meanwhile, settled comfortably into the niche created for him by his father and grandfather before him. Over many generations the Taylors had played a dominant role in the business and political life of the Pale. It required no effort for Francis to slip easily into a world where his name guaranteed him instant deference and political advantage. Through extensive intermarriage the Taylors were related to many other members of the Pale's gentry, and by 1595 Francis was mayor of the City of Dublin. He had meanwhile married Gennet Shelton in yet another marital alliance between Dublin's wealthy citizens, for Gennet's father, Thomas Shelton, was a rich city merchant. The Taylors had six children: Thomas, who was to carry on the family tradition of political involvement, George, Walter, James, Robert and Mary. Francis was a busy man, running a vast estate and developing a career as a political thinker and leader. He kept a very close eye on political developments at home and abroad, for he knew the future was full of ominous signs which could only be met by courage and forthrightness.

Francis' political career started formally at the age of thirty-six when he was selected to be one of Dublin's two sheriffs. It was the official start of a life of public service which spanned the next three decades and was to see him rise to city treasurer, city auditor and finally to mayor in 1595. When the Pale came under pressure from the government and its citizens began to fear for their future, they looked to Francis to articulate their fears and lobby for change. In 1597, he was one of two city agents sent to the English court in London to put Dublin's case to the monarch and the privy council. It was not the kind of job to be entrusted to a political lightweight, and it says much about the esteem in which he was held by his contemporaries. The Pale, and Dublin in particular, were coming very unhappily to terms with the changing political climate. The city's traditional gentry found themselves regarded more and more as politically suspect and saw their power base threatened by the new wave of Protestant settlers and English officials, whose loyalty to Crown and Protestantism was unquestioned.

During the O'Neill wars at the turn of the century, there was an upsurge in Counter-Reformation activity in Dublin, and this did nothing to reassure the Crown authorities about the fidelity of the class which Francis Taylor represented.

Now that O'Neill had been defeated, the government set out to dismantle the control exercised by Catholics in the town councils. The oath of supremacy was rigorously demanded of all public office holders. Anyone who would not acknowledge the English monarch as head of the Church was excluded from holding public positions of power and prominence. It was already a crime not to attend Protestant worship, but the penalty was so small (a fine of twelve old pence) that the wealthy treated the law with contempt. Now the screws tightened, and instead of being prosecuted in the normal courts, Catholics were brought before the Castle Chamber, an informal judicial forum where the normal laws did not apply. Here, handpicked anti-Catholic judges were free to impose whatever punishments short of death they liked. Huge fines and indefinite periods of imprisonment were the sticks used to beat the recusants into abject subjection. What they in fact produced was open and widespread resistance and even greater practice of the Catholic Faith.

The Crown administrators were outraged by the outright disregard of the law and by the fact that the worst offenders were Dublin's leading citizens. They decided to show just how tough the law could be on recusants. Two dozen of Dublin's best known councillors and prosperous burghers were fined very heavily and sentenced to indeterminate prison sentences for their continued practice of the Catholic Faith.

Francis escaped the first round of showcase prosecutions, but his brother-in-law, John Shelton who was elected mayor in 1604, was not permitted to take up the office because he refused to take the oath of supremacy. Instead, a young inexperienced conformist was appointed mayor.

The newcomer was just the kind of person the government wished to reward. The first Irish Parliament since 1585 was about to be elected, and the government was particularly anxious that a majority of its members would be absolutely loyal to the monarchy and Protestantism. There was, however, the rather overwhelming fact that the majority of voters still belonged to the recusant Catholic community. It would take a high degree of skulduggery and threat to deny them their inbuilt domination of the Parliament, but that is what the authorities were determined to do.

Francis Taylor and his fellow members of the city council were not political innocents. They knew what was coming and set about planning carefully for the elections. The civic community was entitled to elect two members to the parliament. Francis was one of a number of aldermen who met in sub-committee to draw up a legislative programme to be brought before the parliament for the good management of the city of Dublin. It was not surprising that when the election took place, Francis was one of two popular and articulate recusants who were chosen for the Parliament.

Francis' election stirred up a vicious hornet's nest. The mayor, a former Catholic who had conformed to Protestantism, had been absent from the city for the vote. On his return, he declared the result null and void and held another poll. This time, conveniently, two Protestants were returned. In the ensuing row, the Protestants took their seats, their Catholic critics were summarily imprisoned, and a royal commission set up to adjudicate the matter fudged its way to an inconclusive outcome in November 1613.

Francis was among those who ended up in prison. There are no records of a prosecution or a trial because he was imprisoned simply by administrative order. The government wanted this pivotal, respected leader off the political scene and effectively disabled. The martyrdom of Conor O'Devany had rebounded furiously on the authorities, and they were not keen to repeat the same mistake with someone of Francis Taylor's stature. It was easier to let him languish in Dublin Castle where the miserable conditions would wear him down slowly and inexorably, as they had done to Margaret Ball twenty years earlier.

For the next seven years, Francis was kept isolated in freezing cold and unmitigated squalor. He died slowly, physically broken by the appalling conditions imposed upon him. Although he had many influential acquaintances only too willing to put pressure on the authorities to release him, Francis was not prepared to buy his way out of prison or surrender his right to practise his faith.

His cell became his chapel. At the very centre of Protestant Dublin, at its most brutal core in the bowels of Dublin Castle, he practised his Catholic Faith in his heart and soul. On 4 January 1621, his health failing rapidly, he was given permission to make his will. His sons George and Robert were present to witness it. The bulk of his estate he left to his son Thomas, like his father a noted and vocal recusant. He was leaving him more than his estate and money. He was more importantly leaving him the baton of faith and the solemn responsibility for carrying the struggle for Catholic freedom into the next generation. He made provision for his wife, left a small sum to the poor, 'in way of devotion for my soules health,' and asked that he be buried in St. Audoen's Church beside his parents.

On the evening of 30th January he sank gently and gladly into the release of death without the remotest trace of bitterness or hatred in his heart. A pathetic squabble ensued between the prison authorities and the Taylor family for the right to bury his body. It was finally resolved, and Francis Taylor, Catholicism's outspoken, courageous and forgiving champion, was buried as he wished in the Church of St. Audoen's. He was already acknowledged throughout the Pale as a distinguished martyr for his faith.

CHAPTER 9

Father Peter Higgins

Dominican Priest,
martyred in Dublin in 1642

One of the saddest features of Peter Higgins' life is that so much of the historical documentation which could have shed light on him was obliterated during the religious persecution of the seventeenth century. No records of Catholic baptisms exist for that period, and the Dominican archives, which would normally be a rich source of information on one of its members, were decimated. The violations committed against individuals and institutions during those dark days were also committed against the generations to come. Instead of a history clearly documented, instead of a story easily told, we have only haphazard accounts and large gaps. It is a measure of Peter Higgins' contribution to the period that despite his consignment to virtual obscurity, his name has managed to survive across the blank pages and unwritten scripts, calling out for vindication, despite the best efforts of those who killed him to ensure that his name would be instantly and forever forgotten. It has slipped somehow through the crevices of time.

Peter Higgins was born in Dublin just at the beginning of the seventeenth century. As a child of recusant parents in the Pale, his earliest memories were probably of the political turmoil created by the wars of the earls and the profound disappointment which seared the Catholic community when they were unexpectedly defeated and fled into exile. From then on, life in the Pale was one large unwieldy mass of uncertainty as the government blew hot and cold on enforcement of the Protestant state religion. Politically Catholics grew more and more marginalised, their power waning year by year. The Old English, many of them still Catholic, managed to hold on to their property, but they no longer had any significant access to positions of influence in the community. Doors were closing all around them. Even those who had embraced Protestantism found themselves distrusted by the government. The new English, those recently arrived to settle in Ireland, whose loyalty to both Crown and Protestantism was not in doubt, were the political favourites. Their star was in the ascendant. The native old Irish, who shared the Catholic faith but little else with the Old English, watched in despair as their property fell victim to plantation by foreign soldiers of fortune. Everything they owned was stripped from them or was in imminent danger of being stripped, to be given as rewards to the Protestant career planters. There was no comfort for them anywhere. Attacked in their homes and in their souls, pushed out of public office, their anger burnt to a furious pitch. They now made common cause with some of their erstwhile enemies among the Old English. The latter's former allegiance to the Crown had previously set them at odds with the old Irish, but it was now well and truly at the breaking point.

Ireland's history at this point is far from straightforward. What had started out as a fight between Protestantism and Catholicism, loyalty to Crown and loyalty to Rome, was now clouded by new issues which further threatened the always vulnerable stability of the island. In Ulster, much of which is now Northern Ireland, the Ulster Scots planters found themselves at odds with the Crown too. Scots Presbyterianism was as detested by the authorities as Catholicism and it too was to feel the violence of persecution. In England, King Charles I faced the wrath of Scotland as well as massive internal political problems as the country slid inexorably into civil war.

The year 1641 is an infamous one in Protestant mythology. Legends still persist about what happened on that fateful October day, with allegations of a huge massacre of Protestants in Ulster embedded deeply in the consciousness of Protestant, even to the present day.

The Catholic people of Ulster had watched as their lands were taken from them by force and handed over to Protestant settlers. They were now second-class citizens in their own country, forced to eke out a living in marginal lands while the best property was enjoyed by strangers. They knew no peace. Their religious faith was outlawed, and everything they did was suspect. After almost a century of merciless bloodletting in the name of enforced Protestantism, the native Irish of Ulster were in an ugly humour indeed. Ironically, it was not the most dispossessed who precipitated the uprising but the relatively well-off Catholic gentry who still held on to their lands, but who were sufficiently distressed about their prospects to unleash a bitter counter-attack.

On 22 October 1641, in a series of lightning raids, some 2,000 Protestant settlers in Ulster were brutally slain. In the widespread tempest of bloodletting that followed upwards of 12,000 Protestants are thought to have been murdered. In the words of historian Roy Foster, "The number of victims killed in the initial 'massacre' rapidly became inflated to fantastic levels, affecting both Irish historiography and Protestant mentality from this time on." The Protestants now had their martyrs and there was a strong fear that this was the beginning of the end for Protestantism in Ireland. The legend grew of a Catholic plot to drive Protestants into the sea and foremost among those suspected of hatching this plot were, inevitably, the Catholic priests.

The insurrection in Ulster had serious consequences throughout the two islands. Scotland held its breath to see if the depredations would hit the Ulster Scots, but the so-called "rebels" had been careful not to rouse that particular monster. The attacks had concentrated on English Protestant settlers. Still, the prospect of a Scottish invasion was one of the volcanic elements in the air, which was thick with the most terrifying possibilities. The reaction in the Pale, to which large numbers of Protestant refugees had fled from Ulster, was crucial. The well-to-do Catholics of Dublin had little sympathy with the insurrectionists, but the government made it crystal clear that all Catholics, even those who claimed to be opposed to the insurrection, were not to be trusted.

The government of the day was in the hands of two Lord Justices, Parsons and Borlase. They were both vehemently puritanical and anti-Catholic. Ignoring the moderate voice of the Earl of Ormond, Protestant (Old English) commander of the army, who cautioned against crude retaliation on the whole Catholic community, the Lord Justices gave their orders to the governor of Dublin, Sir Charles Coote. The situation called for the immediate summary execution of as many "rebels" as could be rounded up. The definition of a rebel was simple: any priest or native Irish person. The poor of the Pale and the Catholic clergy were to pay the price for the October uprising. They were rounded up in droves, among them a priest well-known throughout the Kildare area as one who had given comfort and shelter to many Protestant refugees when they, fearful for their lives as sectarian warfare erupted in pockets across the country, had fled in desperation from their homes.

Peter Higgins had returned to Ireland from Spain during the 1630s. Presumably he had studied for the priesthood abroad and been ordained there. Ireland of the 1630s was enjoying another lull before yet another storm. There was a religious standoff when Lord Deputy Wentworth decided life would be easier all round if people were left to practise their religion as they pleased. His benign tolerance, among other things, did not match the expectations of his peers and betters. In May 1641, Wentworth himself was executed by the very government he had dedicated himself to serve.

In the breathing space created by Wentworth, the Dominicans reopened a monastery in Naas, County Kildare, on part of a site which had been taken from them earlier when the monasteries were dissolved. Peter Higgins settled in there, working as a pastor to the townspeople of Naas and their rural neighbours. In time, he became the prior of the monastery.

In late 1641, panic engulfed the Protestant community throughout Ireland in the wake of the tragic events in Ulster. Government forces vented their anger on innocent Catholics, and they in turn took out their frustration on their Protestant neighbours. The lawlessness eventually reached Naas, driving Protestants from their homes to seek protection in Dublin. Peter Higgins, as prior of the Dominicans in Naas, was in a position to give a lead to others. He was enraged by the sectarian attacks perpetrated by his fellow Catholics, and he denounced them roundly. His energies were channelled into giving what protection and assistance he could to the Protestant refugees in the area. Later, when he faced death himself, those whom he had helped would plead in vain for his life to be spared. One Protestant clergyman told how he was saved from hanging by the timely and courageous intervention of a priest whom he did not know. The evidence pointed strongly to the likelihood that his protector was Peter Higgins.

At the end of January 1642, the Earl of Ormond set out from Dublin leading a contingent of soldiers. Their objective was to restore peace in the Naas area. Peter Higgins presented himself to Ormond, identified himself as a priest and asked for Ormond's protection. The Earl, having no doubt, validated Higgins' claim that he was loyal to the Crown and had actively worked against the rebels by assisting the frightened Protestants, agreed to protect him. Both men knew that as a priest Higgins was likely to be prosecuted no matter how innocent, no matter how loyal to the government. Ormond assured the priest that even if he was charged with an offence, he would be guaranteed a fair jury trial. The Dominican was reassured but almost immediately he became the victim of a power struggle between Sir Charles Coote, the governor of Dublin, and Ormond. Coote had no time for niceties like juries and trials. All Catholics, and in particular all priests, were traitors. Higgins, in his view, had to be executed. For years to come, Ormond would argue to a sceptical public that he fought against this view tooth and nail but that Coote outmanoeuvred him. While Higgins was imprisoned in Dublin, Ormond rounded up exculpatory evidence from two dozen or so Protestants. One after the other they told the Lord Justices that but for Higgins they would have been in mortal peril. Still, Higgins remained in prison. The grave uncertainty which hung over him and the gloom of his prison cell were relieved by several clandestine visits from one of his Dominican superiors, who at great personal risk saw to it that he received the sacraments.

With so much evidence in Higgins' favour, the Lord Justices were at a loss to find something to charge him with. In England, however, a proclamation had been issued on 8th March ordering all Catholic priests to leave the country or face charges of treason. While the decree technically did not apply to Ireland, priests were already finding themselves treated as if it were the law.

Coote seized his opportunity. A shocked public saw Peter Higgins brought to the scaffold in the early morning of 23rd March. There had been no trial, no conviction, no sentence. Word spread rapidly throughout Dublin, a city choking at the seams with displaced refugees, among them many whom Peter Higgins had helped to safety. They gathered in disbelief at the foot of the scaffold. He spoke to them briefly, but even those few words were to create an air of doubt about Ormond's role in his death, a doubt which cast a long shadow over the Ormond family in the years to come. The crowd heard him declare his total allegiance to the king, an allegiance in which he had never wavered, and his commitment to the Catholic Faith and to the Dominican order. He told them of his efforts to save the lives of the unfortunate Protestants of Kildare when they faced mob terror. Among the crowd were some who had reason to know that he spoke the truth. They cried sorely at his death. Others saw only a Catholic priest to mock and jeer at. It was a curious scene. In an audience made up almost exclusively of Protestants, there were those who were heart-broken and those who were triumphant. After Father Higgins died, his body was stripped naked and left to whatever humiliations the crowd devised. It was eventually buried outside the city walls.

Ormond declared that he knew nothing of these events while they were taking place. Some hours after Higgins' death, a relative of Ormond, who had seen the body, told him of the priest's execution. Ormond was beside himself with rage and demanded that Coote should be tried for Higgins' death. The two Lord Justices, Borlase and Parsons, who were probably active accomplices in the execution, refused to entertain the idea.

Ormond was soon to find that Higgins' ringing accusation from the scaffold would colour his relationship with Irish Catholics forever. Although historians find his version of events to be credible, he was thoroughly distrusted by his contemporaries. His enigmatic role in Peter Higgins' death was a significant stumbling block, when later as Lord Lieutenant in 1645 he tried to hammer out a peace treaty.

Hatred of the Catholic Faith was the unadorned motive for putting Peter Higgins to death. Not the remotest taint of succour to the "rebels" ever touched his name. Thirty-eight years after his death, Edmund Borlase, son of Lord Justice Borlase, wrote a history of the rebellion in which he passionately asserted that Higgins was the entirely blameless victim of Coote's "barbarity." In his treatise he was anxious to paint Ormond, and indeed the Lord Justices, in a favourable light. Why he felt the need to do so after the lapse of so many years says something about the potency of Peter Higgins' cruel death. It was an icon. For almost the first time there was a credible body of evidence among the Protestant community testifying to the innocence of the man. The usual mythology of guilt by association, or guilt by virtue of being a priest, was challenged at its very source. Peter Higgins has the distinction of being first acknowledged a martyr for the Catholic faith by the Protestant people to whom he offered the hand of love, friendship and peace.

CHAPTER 10

Terence Albert O'Brien

Bishop of Emly, died in Limerick,
30th October 1651

In the decade between the death of Peter Higgins and his fellow Dominican, Terence O'Brien, Ireland became acquainted with the name of Oliver Cromwell. Few names stir up such deeply conflicting emotions. To Irish Catholics he was the devil incarnate. To some historians he was a model of religious tolerance, England's first republican, the man who crushed the power of the monarchy. Whatever he was, his prejudices and preoccupations were to overwhelm Ireland, drowning it in a sea of blood unparalleled in the hundred years before he landed at Ringsend in Dublin on a fateful August day in 1649.

Cromwell was a little lad of two running about the fields of England's Huntingdon, no doubt playing soldiers, when Terence O'Brien entered the world in 1601. He was born in Tuogh, near Cappamore, County Limerick, in the diocese of Emly. There were few similarities between the two boys. Cromwell was the son of deeply committed Protestant parents who had grown wealthy from the dissolution of the Catholic monasteries. Raised in an environment which was rigidly anti-Catholic, and fanatically religious with a strongly self righteous bent, he came to believe that he was one of God's Chosen. Terence O'Brien, on the other hand, was the son of a wealthy old Irish noble family. He was well educated, but just as Oliver Cromwell was settling down to married life, Terence opted for the life of a celibate priest, a lifestyle thoroughly detested by the soldier of fortune. As Lord Lieutenant and Commander-in-Chief, Cromwell would set in motion the events leading to Terence O'Brien's martyrdom.

The Dominican Order re-established a number of the monasteries which had been destroyed during the Reformation, among them the house in Limerick city which Terence entered as a novice. He joined the Dominicans as an exact contemporary of Peter Higgins. It is inconceivable that the two men were unknown to each other, but though both received their religious formation in Spain, there is no evidence that they studied together. Terence O'Brien studied for the priesthood in Toledo but there were many Dominican seminaries dotted across Spain in those days and it is perfectly possible that both men studied there at the same time without ever crossing each other's paths. Terence had to cope with the loss of his father in 1623, a cross he shared with Oliver Cromwell who had also lost his father in his late adolescence. Terence was ordained in 1627, though whether in Spain or in Ireland is not known for certain. What is certain is that like Peter Higgins, he returned to Ireland to begin his work as a minister of the Gospel.

Father Terence O'Brien was a popular Dominican priest in his home diocese of Emly. He was quickly marked out for his qualities as a leader and organiser, and like Peter Higgins, he had the distinction of becoming prior in the monastery he had entered as a novice many years earlier.

Popular with colleagues and lay people alike, it came as no surprise when he was elected as head of the Dominican Order in Ireland in 1643. His new role took him to Rome the following year for the Order's general chapter. Ironically, one of his tasks there was to present a list of Dominicans who had been martyred for the

Catholic Faith in Ireland. Little did he realise that he was only a few short years away from being on the list himself. For the time being the trip brought a welcome respite from the dangerous political climate of his native Tipperary and also well deserved recognition of his work for the Church. He was awarded the honorary title of Master of Sacred Theology by the Dominican Master General before setting out for home by way of Lisbon, where he visited the famous (and still standing) Irish Dominican convent and monastery. While he was in Lisbon, rumours reached him that he was to be appointed co-adjutor bishop of Emly. A group of influential lay people and senior clerics of the diocese had been lobbying Pope Urban VIII to appoint Terence as co-adjutor. The incumbent bishop was in very poor health and was much too feeble to cope with a diocese which was living through very violent and complex times. Things were sliding dangerously out of control and a firm hand was needed. The people of the diocese wanted Terence O'Brien at the helm. As co-adjutor he would have power to put a steadying hand on diocesan affairs, and when the old bishop died there would be no lapse of continuity. As it happened, the political turmoil of the day caused such a delay in his appointment that the old bishop had been dead for eight months before Terence was consecrated titular bishop of Calama and co-adjutor of Emly, by the then papal nuncio, Archbishop Rinuccini in Waterford city on 2 April 1648. Terence O'Brien was now Bishop of Emly and his problems just beginning.

Irish Catholicism was not a monolithic or homogeneous mass. Within it were sectional and rival interest groups whose unity in the face of a common enemy was always liable to disintegrate. For six years the Catholics of Emly had fought together in often violent confrontations to secure their religious freedom. But when they weren't fighting the "enemy," they were squabbling among themselves. The Old English Catholics wanted religious freedom but they also wanted their previous political and social status restored. The Earl of Ormond offered them an exclusive deal which secured their situation, but did nothing for the old Irish Catholics. The united front collapsed into two bitterly hostile camps with the nuncio and Bishop O'Brien on the side of the old Irish. As the split poisoned the air of every monastery and parish, Ireland turned in on itself, venting its fury in internal dissensions and offering itself on a plate to the opportunistic conqueror Oliver Cromwell.

Cromwell was a new kind of English warlord. Throughout the 1640s, England had suffered from the upheaval of civil war as the autocratic King Charles struggled vainly to hold on to his power. The war contained a number of combustible elements, from internecine warfare between Calvinist and High Church Protestants to high taxation and profligate spending by the king. The entire mess culminated in Charles' execution in January 1649. Among those who signed his death warrant was Oliver Cromwell. The British Isles were declared a Republic and Cromwell was named the first Chairman of the new Commonwealth's Council of State.

He soon turned his attention to Ireland. It was a sitting duck and one which could solve a number of his immediate problems, almost all of which had to do with money. Widespread confiscation of Catholic property in Ireland would settle the arrears in army pay and reward those who had supported the Calvinist party. The legend of the 1641 anti-English uprising in Ulster was grossly and cynically inflated to fuel anti-Catholic hatred among the troops. They set out from Dublin to seize all Catholic property, to push the dispossessed into the barren bleak lands of the far west of Connacht, and to punish all papists who came into their hands. Massacre followed massacre. Priests and people were rounded up and killed indiscriminately. Cromwell was giving full vent to his hatred of the Mass, of priests and of papists in general, and he was doing it in the name and with the authority, as he said, of God himself. The man whose supporters saw in him a religious libertarian was never to reconcile that label with his actions in Ireland. So also his republican and alleged egalitarian credentials would never be reconciled with his authoritarian leadership and his attempts to establish a family dynasty with his espousal of rule by the common man.

Within ten months Ireland had all but collapsed under the weight of the Cromwellian onslaught.

Cromwell himself felt comfortable enough to leave the last pockets of resistance to his son-in-law, Henry Ireton, and in May 1650, he returned to a calamity-stricken England, his name carved like a raw unhealable scar over the landscape of Irish history.

Ireton arrived on the banks of the Shannon at the end of 1650. The city of Limerick blocked further progress and its bridge over the Shannon was a prime target. Inside the city walls a depressed Terence O'Brien was trying to make sense out of the catastrophic events in his country. He consoled himself with the vain hope that Cromwell might be so distracted by events at home in England that he would give Ireland a temporary respite from his marauding and murder. The hope was a vain one. Ireton was outside the city walls and there was no help in sight for the unfortunate Catholics of Limerick.

For five months Ireton besieged the city. Negotiations were stopped and started from time to time, but the terms never varied: Catholicism would not be tolerated and priests would get no mercy. Bishop O'Brien himself was offered an enormous bribe attached to a promise of safe conduct if he would advise the people of Limerick to surrender. The bishop in reply offered to surrender himself to Ireton if the rest of the priests were guaranteed their lives. The siege went on, sapping the energy and resources of the people. Bishop O'Brien was at their side throughout, ministering and caring, preaching the Gospel, counselling forgiveness and courage. Sick with fever and malnourishment, the pathetic citizens of Limerick finally surrendered on 27th October. A small number of ringleaders were given pardons, but no priests, and certainly no bishops, were on the list. Ireton entered the city eager to arrest the Bishop of Emly whose courage and fortitude had kept the siege going for so long. He could not be found. Instead, when Ireton's troops left the city, unknown to them was a new recruit. Hidden among the soldiers, disguised in Cromwellian attire, was Bishop Terence O'Brien.

The Bishop's newfound freedom was short-lived. He made his way to a plague house where victims of the bubonic plague, rampant in Ireland at the time, lay sick and dying. There he ministered openly to them and waited for his tormentors to catch up. They weren't long in finding him. He was chained hand and foot, dragged before a hastily convened court martial and summarily sentenced to death by hanging, simply "for being a priest."

As he waited for the death sentence to be carried out, Bishop O'Brien asked, more in hope than expectation, for the right to be allowed to make his last confession. To his surprise, the request was granted. His fellow Dominican, Denis Hanrahan, visited his cell and gave him absolution. The two men were very old friends. They had been together in Spain and had both endured the long hard days of the siege of Limerick. O'Brien was reconciled to his approaching death and not at all bitter, but he told Father Hanrahan that at his court martial he had prophesied that death was coming to Henry Ireton too.

On 30th October, the morning after his trial, Terence Albert O'Brien stood in front of the gallows surrounded by a crowd of defeated and dejected Catholics, their hearts distraught by so much death, so much suffering, and so little pity. He was moved by their plight and their goodness in standing by him while he faced the ordeal of hanging. He spoke lovingly of the many disasters and storm clouds which had made their life so hard, but begged them to keep their hearts up and to hold fast to their faith in God. He asked them to pray that he would face his death firmly and with dignity, and it seems that is exactly what he did.

His body was beaten with muskets until its human form was so distorted that it was impossible to say what species of animal it was. His head was cut off and left on a spike by the river's edge to be reviled and mocked. As the days went on and the head was seen to stay fresh, the mocking ceased and was replaced by silence and wonder. No other priest arrested along with him suffered the same indignities as Bishop O'Brien. When Henry Ireton died a short time later, he was said to have suffered an agonising delirium as the memory of Bishop O'Brien's shameful death haunted his final days and hours.

CHAPTER 11

Father John Kearney

Franciscan Priest, died at Clonmel,
County Tipperary, 11th March 1653

The Cromwellian vortex of death continued. Henry Ireton was barely cold in his grave when Charles Fleetwood succeeded him, not only as Commander-in-Chief of the English forces in Ireland but also as husband of Bridget Cromwell. She certainly had a knack of picking rabidly anti-Catholic husbands, for Fleetwood was, if anything, worse than his predecessor. Now that Ireland was utterly defeated, her people beaten into the ground, the mopping up operation began, its objective to rid the country once and for all of any trace of Catholicism. Once more, the prime victims were priests. Foremost among them was a young Franciscan named John Kearney. By the time he faced his own martyrdom, he was no stranger either to suffering or to the crude racist brutality that engulfed his people.

John Kearney was born in the beautiful County Tipperary town of Cashel. Few Irish towns have as pretty a setting or as stunning a rural hinterland, and John Kearney was doubly blessed in that he was not born into abject poverty like the majority of his fellow citizens but into a rich merchant family whose involvement with Cashel life went back many generations. The Kearneys were related through marriage to virtually all the well-to-do families of the area and John was only one of a number of priests produced by this large and devoutly Catholic clan. John's parents and relations were steeped in the Counter-Reformation, their daily lives a shining example of commitment and devotion to the Catholic Faith, no matter what the political winds dictated or politics favoured. They were fortunate that in their territory of South Tipperary there was always very strong pastoral support from the local priest, among whom were Jesuits and Franciscans, as well as diocesan priests.

Both the Franciscans and the Jesuits were active in Cashel when John Kearney was growing up, and each had a hand in his education. The Franciscan monastery had been dissolved in 1540, but in 1618 the friars returned quietly and opened a friary in an undistinguished private house. From there they visited the homes of the faithful, giving religious instruction to the children. Young John, a daily communicant from the age of six, attended the Jesuit school. When he made up his mind that he had a vocation to the priesthood, he faced an agonising choice between the Society of Jesus, to which he was intellectually attracted, and the Franciscans whom his parents favoured and to whom he was emotionally and spiritually drawn. Over the years his family home had often been the scene of clandestine drama, when fugitive priests were smuggled in under cover of darkness to protect them from marauding soldiers. It was a dangerous business, but it had become almost a routine way of life for the Kearneys. Taking risks for the Faith was therefore nothing new to John, but was rather part of the ethos his parents were eager to cultivate in him.

Among those who had been hidden from time to time at the Kearney house and who had reason to be grateful for their courage and hospitality was Father Joseph Everard, Minister Provincial of the Friars Minor. After a long discussion with Father Everard about his dilemma, John chose the Franciscans and set out with his like-minded best friend, Joseph Sail, for the friary at Kilkenny.

After a short period in the novitiate and following the custom of the era, the two young men set off for St. Anthony's
College in Louvain, which had been founded thirty years earlier by the Irish Franciscans. They arrived in Belgium in 1638
after a horrendous sea journey and began their preparation for
the priesthood. Four happy years passed studying theology and
philosophy, and on 20 September 1642, John Kearney was ordained by the Archbishop of Mechlin, Jacobus Boonen, in the
church of St. Catherine's in Brussels. After ordination he stayed
on in Louvain for another two years while he completed his
studies, and in the late summer of 1644 he said goodbye to
Belgium and his student days. His apprenticeship was over and
it was time to go home. The storms which made such a misery
out of his first sea journey to Belgium were only a pale shadow
of the misfortunes which began with his homecoming.

By sheer bad luck the ship carrying Father John Kearney back
home was set upon and captured by English Parliamentarians.
They put into harbour in Bristol and John was taken to London
under arrest. His prompt and open acknowledgment of the fact
that he was a priest earned him three months of torture and finally
a death sentence. As he sat in his dungeon on the night before
the sentence was to be carried out, a sympathetic English Catholic
helped him to escape and got him safely on a boat to France. His
miraculous escape gave him only a brief respite, but he must have
been a very happy man to see the dock in Calais.

After a short stay in France, he set sail again for Ireland. This
time he arrived without incident and made his way joyfully to
Cashel. There, a reunion with family and friends blotted out the
memory of the long anguished nights in an English prison where
the simple renunciation of his faith would have ended the beatings
and given him freedom. Now he was home, among those whose
faith had sustained him, and whose training and example he had

struggled to keep in front of him in times of pain and weakness. For the time being, he joined the local friary as a teacher of philosophy.

The faith he nourished and now shared with the young friars in Cashel had grown strong in adversity, but nothing prepared it for the harrowing tests it was to face after a brief lull. He was a formidable and popular preacher, something of a local "star," and his superiors were plagued by requests from all over the county for him to preach.

Sometime around 1647, John Kearney was transferred to Waterford city where he became Novice Master and had considerable scope as a preacher. Once again he just missed death by inches, for in the same year he left Cashel, Elizabeth Creagh, his mother, was murdered when Murrough O'Brien, Lord Inchiquin, annihilated the Cashel garrison. Clergy and people sought shelter in the cathedral. They were pursued and relentlessly mowed down by the Gaelic chieftain, now Protestant, Royalist and Catholic hater. O'Brien was hellbent on profiting as much as he could by taking advantage of the political crisis and grabbing Munster for himself. The winds of fortune were not always at his back, however, as they appeared to be on that blood-filled day on the Rock of Cashel when the pitiful screams of women and children tore the air asunder. Were they still echoing in O'Brien's head nine years later when life was less kind to him, and in exile from his country he converted to Catholicism?

No record exists of how John Kearney took the news of his mother's murder. He knew many of those killed along with her, childhood friends, fellow priests, cousins, students and neighbours. The community from which he came had been devastated in one squall of brutality, and if his heart burned with anger and screamed for vengeance as many human hearts did, it would have been at least understandable. But the young Franciscan had faced that anger in varying degrees before, had tempered it with Christ's steadying hand and had risen above it. He continued to preach, comforting the terrified people with words of hope and offering forgiveness and love to those whose malice was poisoning the country.

On 24 November 1649, Cromwell's soldiers arrived at the doors of Waterford and demanded the city's surrender. The news of their carnage at Drogheda and Wexford preceded them, and Waterford could not expect anything better than the treatment already meted out elsewhere. John Kearney knew time was running out for him as well. Now the priest whose family had willingly risked their lives to save endangered clerics was forced to take refuge himself. His priestly ministry changed dramatically. From a public preacher he became an almost ghostly figure, appearing silently in homes throughout the area, bringing the Gospel and the sacraments to a people who were on the verge of total despair. At the time the country was ravished as much by plague as it was by politics, and those who were ill became the subject of John Kearney's special ministry. He moved between plague houses, heedless of all the physical dangers that surrounded him, his gentle care for the sick becoming as legendary as his former reputation as a preacher.

Cromwell's campaign had unleashed such a level of bloodshed and terror that the Catholic bishops met urgently at Clonmacnois in December 1649, to assess the situation. They accused Cromwell of planning to remove every trace of Catholicism from Ireland. In reply Cromwell made it plain that he and the bishops were in agreement on that much at least. He loathed the Mass, and would not tolerate it. He loathed papists, and would hunt them down. As for priests, their elimination would be a special concern of his as he went about God's work.

John Kearney's secret work continued until the summer of 1650 when the Franciscan Friars Minor managed to hold a provincial chapter at the monastery in Kilconnell. Many of their priests were dead or on the run. Waterford city had just surrendered to the

Cromwellian army on 6th August. With the city now in English hands, John Kearney could not return to Waterford. Instead, he was named as Guardian of the nearby friary at Carrick-on-Suir. It was no haven of safety. One by one the towns of County Tipperary fell to the invading army until there was not a church left in the county. No priest was safe. Some headed for France and John Kearney found himself under pressure from relatives and friends to get out of Ireland while he could. No amount of coaxing or cajoling could induce him to go. He had a clear and immovable vision of his vocation in these troubled times, and it was to be with the suffering people, bringing them the comfort of the sacraments and being ready day or night to suffer along with them. His work continued feverishly and at all hours. There was precious little time for rest, and no time at all when the threat of discovery was absent. In darkened rooms, in strange houses night after night he blessed the water and wine, broke the Sacred Bread, and offered Mass in almost silent murmurings for friends and supporters whose lives were wracked by the misery of uncertainty and the ever-present threat of death. His fearlessness touched them, his Masses gave them strength.

Cromwell was meanwhile drafting a plan for a new civil administration for a new Ireland cleansed of Catholicism. The country was divided into precincts, each with its own military governor. The Tipperary town of Clonmel was to be the headquarters of one precinct. Government was conducted by four commissioners, and among their first edicts was a proclamation banishing all priests from Ireland within twenty days. It was dated 6 January 1663 and was published in Clonmel two weeks later.

John Kearney remained in hiding, but the penalties for giving him shelter were now so severe that he was reluctant to burden anyone with the danger. It was increasingly difficult to evade capture, and in early March he was arrested in Cashel by a Cromwellian search party. He ended up in jail in Clonmel, surrounded by the familiar faces of fellow Franciscans. With death just around the corner, they used their time to prepare for it, hearing each other's confession, giving absolution and saying Mass.

Next morning he was brought before a court to face a battery of charges. His accusers claimed he had celebrated Mass and administered the sacraments throughout the province of Munster. He had strengthened Catholics in their faith and impeded their conversion from popery to the true Protestant religion. The young Franciscan answered that the allegations were absolutely true. After all, he was a Catholic priest. The accusations merely stated that he did the job he was expected to do. The courtroom atmosphere was menacing, with threats emanating from the bench throughout the proceedings. John Kearney was defiant and unshakeable. He accused his accusers of administering unjust laws. The trial judge, Viscount Sankey, predictably found him guilty of "functioning as a Catholic priest in defiance of the law." All those tried that same day were sentenced to banishment. John alone was sentenced to death. His unapologetic attitude had clearly irritated Sankey.

At 11 a.m. next morning, wearing his Franciscan habit openly for the first time in many months, he walked to the street corner known today as Martyr's Lane, where the scaffold had been erected. He carried a cross in his hand and his Franciscan rosary dangled from his belt. Kneeling at the foot of the scaffold, he prayed quietly and wept for a few moments. At the top of the steps he was composed and calm enough to tell a half hostile crowd that he was dying for his faith and for no other reason. The charges against him were, he said, that he was a priest, engaged in his priestly duties. "I profess my faith in the Catholic Church, the one true church. I willingly die for it, relying confidently on the merits of Christ."

His last words were barely said when the noose was placed over his head and the platform dropped. His friends asked Sankey for permission to take the body for burial. Sankey was anxious to be rid of the affair as quickly as possible and agreed. Father Kearney's grave was to be in the chapter hall of the suppressed Franciscan frairy in his hometown of Cashel, and the funeral cortege set off on the journey from Clonmel. Before the body reached its resting place, the crowd was already claiming that John's first miraculous cure had occurred along the road. His fame as a martyr was instantaneous and the story of his death, along with relics taken from the habit he wore on the scaffold, were brought to France by his fellow priests. The relics were credited with numerous miracles, and devotion to John Kearney was fostered and grew in those early years after his death. A small package of Kearney's relics found its way to St. Anthony's College in Louvain, where he had been so happy as a student priest. They remained there until 1797, when they were moved for safekeeping. After a number of moves, they finally arrived in Ireland. Since 1947, the fragile folds of seventeenth century paper which surround the little piece of grey cloth and hemp from John Kearney's tunic have been preserved in the Franciscan Library at Killiney near Dublin. Barely legible are the words written on the front of the ageing package: "Ex tunica, ... chorda, et capillis F. Joannis Carneii cuius vitam et martyrium . . ." The rest has been obliterated by time.

CHAPTER 12

Father William Tirry

Augustinian Priest, martyred in Clonmel,
County Tipperary, 2nd May 1654

T he strength of the Catholic Counter-Reformation in Ireland
owed a lot to the dedication and resilience of the Catholic
merchant and business classes who formed its core of support. Not only did they fund it and promote it, but more often
than not it was their sons who became the next generation of young
priests. The bonds which united these families were strengthened by
intermarriage, by shared practice of the faith, and by the common
bond of suffering which they experienced so frequently. Many of
the martyrs were raised in such families, among them William Tirry.

He was born in Cork city in 1608 to a successful merchant family in which religious practice played a central role in everyday life.
His father's brother, after whom he was named, was bishop of the
dioceses of Cloyne and Cork from 1622 until 1646, and the house
was a hive of Counter-Reformation comings and goings. William's
vocation to the priesthood was welcomed and encouraged, though
of course it meant a long time abroad. Catholic education was
illegal in Ireland, and when young William decided to join the
Augustinian Fathers, he left Cork for Valladolid in Spain.

His theological studies took him to the College des Grands
Augustins in Paris, where he passed several years. A short stay in

Brussels completed his education on the European mainland, and towards the end of the 1630s he was back in Ireland again living with the Augustinian community in Cork. His uncle, the bishop of Cork and Cloyne, asked him to stand in for a short period as his secretary. The job lasted four months and William was happy to see it over and to be back with his Augustinian confreres. His stay was short, for now it was his Aunt Joan, the bishop's sister, who was keen to have him as chaplain to her husband and tutor to their sons. Her husband, in one of those quixotic ironies so typical of the time, was the bearer of a name associated in previous generations with anti-Catholic activities rather than Counter-Reformationism. He was the Viscount Kilmallock, otherwise known as Dominic Sarsfield.

From the outset of the Civil War in 1641 until the end of the decade Cork was controlled by the Protestants of Munster. There was no hope of any Augustinian working there openly. William's role as chaplain to the Kilmallock family continued until 1646, when he was appointed as 'socius' to the new Augustinian Provincial, Denis O'Driscoll. The two men travelled together during the next three years meeting with fellow Augustinians just returning from abroad and supporting those who were having difficulty coping with the hazards they encountered in Ireland. They were thus kept informed about political and religious affairs at home and abroad.

In June 1649, William was appointed prior of the monastery at Skryne, County Meath (birthplace of another martyr, Margaret Ball), but before he could make the long journey northwards from his base at Fethard, County Tipperary, Cromwell had landed and Skyrne became virtually inaccessible.

As Cromwellian troops overran the island moving south, Father Tirry went underground for safety. A relative by marriage, Mrs Amy Everard, widow of a wealthy member of the gentry, offered him a refuge in her home. She had one surviving son, whom William tutored, and the house became a centre to which the faithful came secretly for Mass and the sacraments. Unable to engage in a more active ministry because of the tight grip exercised by the soldiers, William spent his time in prayer, fasting and penance. He had a strong inclination to asceticism, so the privacy and seclusion of the Everard home suited him well, but he was aware, particularly after the proclamation of 1653 banishing priests, that every prayer might be in preparation for his imminent death.

There was a price on the head of every priest and a reward of five pounds for anyone giving information leading to a priest's capture. At the time, Ireland had as little difficulty producing informers as she had priests. No less than three people vied to get the reward for disclosing William's whereabouts. As he vested to say Mass on Easter Saturday 1654, the soldiers arrived to arrest him. He was another candidate for the jails in Clonmel.

William expected and prepared for the worst. In the month before his trial, he used every available moment for prayer. A contemporary eyewitness to his behaviour in prison was Franciscan priest Matthew Fogarty who wrote this account of Tirry's imprisonment and death:

> ". . . every morneing betwixt 3 and 4 of the cloke he would get up roundlie and put on his apparell with all expedition, and soon after fall to his prayers on his knees, and there continue till 8th a cloke still either praying, weeping or streekinge his breast through sensible contrition, to the great edification of all his fellow prisoners, to the admiration and conversion to a beter life of all the hearers, both ecciesiasticall and laymen, yea sectaries and papists not onlie in the towne of Clonmel but also further in the townes and villages throughout all Ireland, as far as the bruite and rumour of his holy life were spread."

William Tirry and Matthew Fogarty were tried together before a jury. Fogarty was amazed at William's lack of nervousness and his presence of mind under insistent cross examination. When Paris the judge asked him, ". . . do you acknowledge any higher power in this kingdom than our power?" Fogarty says he answered without any ambiguity or evasion:

> "In temporall matters I acknowledge noe higher power in this kingdome of Ireland than yours ... but in spirituall affaires wherin my soule is concerned I acknowledge the Pope of Rome and myne owne Superiors to have greater power over me than you others."

The jury was instructed to find him guilty of high treason since he had practised as a priest in defiance of the proclamation. He was sentenced to death by hanging. Father Matthew Fogarty, a great deal more nervous and more uncomfortable in court, got precisely the same treatment and sentence.

They were only days away from execution, and Father Tirry wanted to spend the time by himself in prayer, but his reputation as a saintly, holy man drew crowds of men and women outside the jail. As a result, the Marshall, Richard Rous, brought William and his fellow priests to his own home and left them in the charge of a pious priest, Walter Conway, so that all those who wanted to see and hear them could do so. In spite of the crowds, Father Tirry lay prostrate on the floor offering prayer after prayer and asking God to forgive him his sins. Six days and nights he passed in a such a meditative state that he seemed to be already in the company of Christ. When the jailer came to call out the names of those due for execution, Matthew Fogarty was stunned to discover that his name had been omitted. William Tirry heard his own name and rousing himself from his deepest thoughts, he knelt and thanked God "who chosed me to this happie end."

The prison officials were uncomfortable in the presence of so strong and strange a character, yet they too were moved to treat him with a caution that bordered on reverence. Rous ensured that a priest was available to Father Tirry up to the hour of his execution, and he himself put on the manacles by which he was to be led through the streets. The place of execution was the same spot where young John Kearney had welcomed death a year before. This time, the scene was different. John Kearney had faced a subdued and even hostile crowd, among whom were gangs of jeering Cromwellian soldiers. William Tirry made his way slowly through streets lined with people who had come out of respect for his name and his holiness. They wept freely as he went past, blessing them constantly. Several times he knelt to pray, in imitation of Christ's stations of the Cross. By the time he reached the gallows, Marshall Rous was beside himself with distress and treated his prisoner with the utmost courtesy and gentleness. He handed Father Tirry the halter. The priest embraced it and smiled happily at him, saying he was more grateful to receive it than the best chain of gold in the kingdom. He mounted the steps with solemn deliberation at each one, meditating aloud on the ten commandments and the seven sacraments. It was a long time since he or any priest had been free to address so large and so public a crowd. William Tirry took full advantage of it, much to the annoyance of a Protestant minister who had looked on silently at first, but whose fury at what he was hearing, and its obvious effect on the crowd, provoked him into haranguing the condemned man. Before William could reply, Marshal Rous intervened to berate the minister and to assure the priest that he was free to continue his speech. Father Tirry asked simply that if any priest of his own Order were present, he would be grateful to receive absolution. He signalled to Mr Rous to do his duty.

Later, when Father Matthew Fogarty (whose sentence had been commuted to banishment) had the chance to meet Amy Everard and tell her about the devout and prayerful way her erstwhile lodger had prepared for death, she remarked that even before he had any prospect of death his rich and relentless prayer life had been no different.

Father Tirry's burial at the Augustinian Friary in Fethard was not the cloak-and-dagger affair that often accompanied the deaths of priests, with bodies being spirited away and quietly buried by a few brave faithful. If Cromwell had wanted to know how successful his scorching and torching of Catholicism was, he need only have observed the open ceremonial burial of Father William Tirry. This man's prayerful witness was his legacy to his own tired generation and to its children, born into a century in which the demise of Irish Catholicism was among the political ambitions of the English government. Each of the martyrs in his or her own way ensured that this ambition remained unfulfilled. Quite what they would make of twenty-first century Ireland, twenty-first century Christianity, the twenty-first century Catholic Church is a matter for open debate, a debate worth having.

ACKNOWLEDGMENTS

The extensive formal documentation (positio) which led to the beatification of the sixteen men and one woman who are the subjects of this book was prepared by the late Monsignor John Hanly and Fr Gerry Rice. When I started this project, three decades ago first as a video and then as this text, both men were very generous with their help, encouragement and liberal access to their papers. I am hugely indebted to them and hope their work will one day be vindicated in the canonisations they worked so diligently to promote. I am also grateful to two men who have close associations with my favourite Irish village, Rostrevor, County Down. Historian Dr John McCavitt's wise professional guidance was invaluable and Latinist Rev. Canon Michael Hackett provided willing help with translations. I acknowledge also the personal support I received from the late Cardinal John Joseph O'Connor in pursuing these narratives. A special word of thanks to Garry O'Sullivan of Columba Book who helped me bring to publication and to life, a text which has been sitting on my desk for much too long but waiting for what I hope is the right time.